OPENING DOORS

THE ADMINISTRATOR'S GUIDE TO THE
SCHOOLWIDE ENRICHMENT MODEL

Nora G. Friedman

Dedication

This work is dedicated to my sons, Andy and Jon.
Follow your dreams.

Editor:

Rachel A. Knox

Cover Illustration:

Andy Friedman

ISBN: 0-936386-98-3

Creative Learning Press, Inc., P.O. Box 320, Mansfield Center, CT 06250
888-518-8004 • www.creativelearningpress.com

Acknowledgements

This book represents my personal quest for the best methods for implementing SEM. I wish to express my heartfelt thanks and gratitude to the many wonderful people who helped me along the way. I am most grateful to Dr. Joseph Renzulli for being my mentor for almost twenty years. His wisdom has shaped my life in ways that are difficult to explain. Thanks also goes to Dr. Sally Reis, who is a remarkable person and educator. She compelled me to think deeply about my work, and her insights throughout the writing of this book and for the many years I have known her have been an inspiration to me.

My editor Rachel Knox kept me focused and on course and without her extreme patience and encouragement, I doubt the final product would achieve the high standard of which I am most proud.

Special thanks goes to the many administrators who participated in the interviews and remained in close contact with me, willing to share their experiences and materials, particularly Ellen Agostinelli. Deb Goldbeck and Lee Ann Cervini offered me support by reading the manuscript and making valuable suggestions. In addition, I owe a great deal to all of my Confratute friends and colleagues who saw value in this work and pressed me onward.

I would also like to thank the Syosset Board of Education and Dr. Carole G. Hankin, Superintendent of Schools in Syosset, New York, for giving me the privilege of working in a school district that values the individuality and interests of each and every youngster. And to my extraordinary staff at the South Grove Elementary School and Michele Webb, our enrichment specialist, thank you for taking the vision of the school district and making it come alive for the boys and girls who attend our school.

My deep gratitude goes to my elementary and junior high school art teacher, Mrs. Barnett, who is no longer in this world, but who deserves a heartfelt thanks for the legacy that she passed on to me. My most sincere appreciation goes to my family: to Millie and Sammy, my parents, who always, always pushed me to do my best; to my sister Marcia, my best friend and soul mate whose support has never wavered; to my sons, Andy and Jon, who have inspired me and taught me about life and all it has to offer; and most importantly, to my husband Bernie and his alter ego Barry, who has taught me more about the joy of living than can ever be expressed in words.

TABLE OF CONTENTS

List of Figures

List of Tables

FOREWORD

Developing the Giftedness and Talents of Young People: A Critical National Priority

The traditional purposes of schooling have been to socialize the young, teach particular forms of knowledge that will bring about a realistic and rational view of the world, and prepare citizens to participate in the democratic way of life. These purposes reflected the needs of societies dominated by the industrial revolution, and in many ways, schools were prototypes of the factories for which they were preparing students. Although these purposes are still important today, changes taking place in the post-industrial world are forcing us to reexamine some of the historical roots of education set forth by progressive educators who viewed learning as a vehicle to unleash the creative potential of young people and to develop leaders who can shape society, not merely participate in it. Early leaders such as Rousseau and Pestalozzi and more contemporary theorists such as Piaget and Dewey called attention to the importance of fulfilling the individual potential of each child and modifying educational strategies that reflect the broad range of abilities, interests, motivation, learning styles, and expression styles that are unique to individual learners.

As we begin a new century, it is a good time to reconsider the purposes of schooling and the things that educational leaders can do to prepare young people for creative and productive lives in a rapidly changing world. Everyone has a stake in good schools because schools create and recreate a successful modern society. Renewed and sustained economic growth; the development of intellectual, creative, and social capital; and the well-being of all citizens requires investing in high-quality learning the same way that previous generations invested in machines and raw materials. As we move toward a post-industrial world, creativity, inventiveness, entrepreneurship, and concerns about social well-being will determine which nations initiate ideas and provide the leadership for continued productivity and, indeed, even preserve a democratic way of life.

The approach to talent development described in this book is designed to help administrators and educators maximize opportunities for creativity, inventiveness, and scientific and artistic pursuits in young people, many of whom will become leaders in all aspects of our nation's growth and development. Each school has a role to play in developing the talent potentials of all students, and educational leaders play a crucial role in creating the conditions in which talent, creativity, innovativeness, and leadership are as valued as traditional achievement.

This book presents an administrator's-eye view of a plan that has demonstrated its effectiveness in bringing about significant changes in schooling. That plan, the Schoolwide Enrichment Model (SEM), is a systematic set of strategies for increasing student effort, enjoyment, and performance and for integrating a broad range of advanced level learning experiences and higher order thinking skills into any curricular area, course of study, or pattern of school organization. The general approach of the SEM is one of infusing more effective practices into existing school structures rather than replacing the ways in which schools are organized and operated. This research-supported plan is designed for general education, but it is based on instructional methods and curricular practices that originated in special programs for high-ability students. It was within the context of these programs that the thinking skills movement and the focus on creative productivity first gained acceptance and provided opportunities for research that verified the effectiveness of learning experiences specifically designed to promote higher levels of thinking and creativity.

Research opportunities in a variety of special programs allowed us to develop instructional procedures and programming alternatives that emphasize the need to (a) provide a broad range of advanced level enrichment experiences for all students and (b) use varied student responses to these experiences as stepping stones for relevant follow-up. This approach is not viewed as a new way to identify who is or is not "gifted." Rather, the process simply identifies how educators can provide subsequent opportunities, resources, and encouragement to support continuous escalations of student involvement in both required and self-selected activities. This approach to developing high levels of multiple potentials in young people is purposefully designed to sidestep the traditional practice of labeling some students "gifted" (and by implication, relegating all others to the category of "not-gifted"), an orientation that has denied many students opportunities to develop high levels of creativity and productivity. (Lay persons and professionals at all levels have begun to question the efficacy of programs that rely on IQ scores and other cognitive ability measures as the primary methods for identifying which students can benefit from differentiated services.)

Practices that have been a mainstay of many special programs for "the gifted" are being absorbed into general education by reform models designed to upgrade the performance of all students. This integration of gifted program know-how is a favorable development for two reasons. First, adopting special program practices underscores the viability and usefulness of both the know-how of special programs and the role enrichment can and should play in total school improvement. Second, *all* students should have opportunities to develop higher order thinking skills and to pursue more rigorous content and first-hand investigative activities than those typically presented in today's knowledge-oriented textbooks. Educators should use the ways in which students *respond* to general experiences as a rationale for providing highly motivated students with advanced level follow-up opportunities. This approach reflects a democratic ideal that accepts the full range of individual differences in the entire student population, and it opens the door to programming models that develop the talent potentials of many at-risk students who traditionally have been excluded from anything but the most basic types of curricular experiences.

Educational leaders have a commitment to understanding diversity in students and in helping students to acquire learning skills in multiple areas. We are delighted that a guidebook designed specifically for principals and other school and district leaders is available and that it is written by a person who has "been there" through all the challenges and creative solutions that make good programs work. And we are even more delighted with the remarkable kinds of teacher growth that have resulted from leadership provided by Nora Friedman as she has gone about implementing SEM programs in a number of schools. When it comes to general school improvement and the development of individual potentials, we believe that a rising tide lifts all ships, and the Schoolwide Enrichment Model is a planned and systematic vehicle for raising the tide for both students and the educators who must grow in the same ways we expect young people to grow.

Joseph S. Renzulli and Sally M. Reis
The National Research Center on the Gifted and Talented
The University of Connecticut

January 2005

PREFACE

When I was a child, my teachers thought I was a "bright little girl" who was not achieving to her potential, and they seized every opportunity to indicate this to my parents. In the hope of inspiring me, the administrators placed me in a homogeneous group of bright youngsters, all white and all from "the better part of town." This cluster of classmates remained together through all of our elementary and junior high school years. Despite this intervention, my parents usually returned from the annual teacher's conference with disappointment in my lack of attention to my studies and perceived unwillingness to work to my potential.

Although I was intelligent and listening, my inability to focus coupled with my learning differences made me appear disinterested. I often used my time to daydream. I spent countless hours doodling, drawing intricate designs all over the margins of my papers. My art teacher took notice of me and others like me and began a Friday afternoon club for students interested in art. The experiences I enjoyed in that art club changed the direction of my life. I began to recognize that school could be a place where interests and talents can be nurtured given the right circumstances. I went on to a specialized public art and academic high school in New York City, where I was given the opportunity to develop my true love for learning and acquire intrinsic motivation. The recognition and development of my artistic talent had a profound effect on my future academic success.

I often think back to the gifts I received from that very special individual, my art teacher, who mentored me toward the success and fulfillment I enjoy today. My experience pushed me to contemplate the gifts I could bring to children just like me. I realized that many children would never have the opportunities I had at that critical point of my learning life. Children from different socio-economic backgrounds or ethnicities are often not placed in "gifted" classes. The passion to touch a young person's life in a meaningful way took root. In my gratitude to this very special educator, I began to think about a career in education to carry on the legacy she passed to me.

I am a product of opportunity and expectation. I have a deep need to support and advocate for students with non-traditional learning styles. Over my twenty-five years as an educator, the children I have known possess gifts and talents well beyond a narrowly defined conception of giftedness. Apart from my observations as a teacher and administrator, I have only to reflect upon my own childhood and schooling experiences to recognize that a narrow definition misses its mark and underserves children. My deep belief in talent development for all children has been fostered by the work of Drs. Joseph Renzulli and Sally Reis. These practical theorists and educators have had a positive impact on school experiences worldwide. Their work enabled me to provide what I believe to be improved classroom learning experiences for many more students.

When I made the decision to become an administrator fifteen years ago and to implement SEM in my school, I found that I wanted more guidance to bring the theory underlying schoolwide enrichment to reality. I set upon a journey to uncover how administrators went about the work of implementing schoolwide enrichment in their schools, and this book brings together what I have learned from my own experiences as well as the hundreds of interviews I conducted with other SEM administrators.

Throughout the text you will find case studies and quotes that emphasize or illustrate a point. These quotes are the words of administrators who believe in SEM and have worked hard to build a program in their schools. Also in the margins, I have highlighted texts that provide additional information or activities about a topic. Appendix D provides full bibliographic information on these as well as other books, articles, and videos that you may find helpful.

I have also included a series of professional development activities to help administrators introduce teachers to SEM and obtain their support, work with the media, and celebrate successes. You should feel free to modify these, as well as sample letters, memos, and flyers that appear throughout the text to suit your own needs. It is my hope that administrators will feel comfortable taking ideas from this manual and molding them to fit their particular programs and schools. In that sense, each manual will always be a work in progress, a collaboration between administrators and those in their school community striving to meet the needs of their students.

1

AN OVERVIEW OF THE
SCHOOLWIDE ENRICHMENT MODEL

The Schoolwide Enrichment Model (SEM) is a research-supported model based on highly successful practices rooted in special programs for gifted and talented students, namely the Enrichment Triad Model (Renzulli, 1977).[1] The model addresses total school improvement through a continuum of services that target student learning needs at every level. SEM does not replace a school's existing services for high-ability students. Instead, it both infuses the high-end learning experiences usually reserved for a few gifted students into the regular curriculum and continues to engage high-ability students who need more rigorous challenges. The model is flexible enough to allow each school to form its own program based on local considerations (resources, student populations, leadership, faculty) and input from stakeholders (teachers, parents, students). The following features characterize SEM programs:

- High standards and advanced levels of academic challenge for all students
- A flexible approach to curriculum modification that accommodates individual needs
- Responsiveness to the needs of low achieving students by replacing traditional remedial methods with an enrichment approach used successfully for years with higher achieving students
- Development of motivation, creativity, thinking skills, and cooperativeness by taking student interests and learning styles into consideration
- A hands-on approach to enrichment that focuses on the use, rather than assimilation, of information and the student's role as a first-hand inquirer

---

[1] Appendix A includes a detailed description of the development of SEM.

- A guarantee of faculty ownership and involvement through a comprehensive planning process that includes teachers, administrators, and specialists

(Renzulli & Reis, 2001)

Figure 1.1 offers a graphic representation of the model's various structures and components for meeting the needs of all students.

SEM Components and Structures

The organizational components of SEM are the resources used to promote program development. Strategies for enhancing parental and community involvement, professional development materials, and staff communication and teaming processes are all organizational components. The school structures include all areas of the regular curriculum, enrichment experiences known as enrichment clusters, and a continuum of services that can range from general enrichment

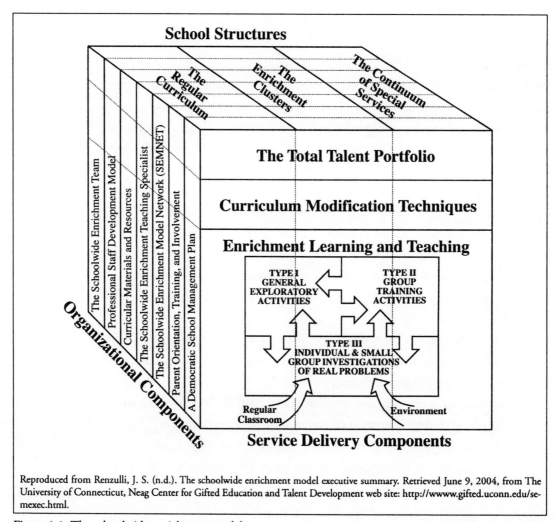

Reproduced from Renzulli, J. S. (n.d.). The schoolwide enrichment model executive summary. Retrieved June 9, 2004, from The University of Connecticut, Neag Center for Gifted Education and Talent Development web site: http://www.gifted.uconn.edu/semexec.html.

Figure 1.1. The schoolwide enrichment model.

within the classroom setting to mentor and internship experiences for students. The service delivery components are the direct services to students and form the core of the model.

Service Delivery Components

The service delivery components—The Total Talent Portfolio, curriculum modification techniques, and enrichment learning and teaching strategies—are at the heart of the model. These components help identify each student's strengths, talents, interests, and current knowledge base, thus providing educators with a foundation for determining appropriate educational experiences for students.

Using the Total Talent Portfolio, educators compile traditional and performance based assessments to get a complete picture of student ability, talent, and interest. This information then enables teachers to focus on student strengths rather than deficits when making decisions about instruction.

Curriculum modification techniques help accommodate students who come into the classroom with different levels of knowledge. Teachers first identify what students already know and what they need to learn for any given unit of study. For students who have already mastered some part of the curriculum or who have the potential to move through the curriculum more quickly than others, teachers then compact the curriculum to allow these students to engage in in-depth learning experiences.

The Enrichment Learning and Teaching service delivery component draws on three types of enrichment experiences: Type I (general exploratory activities), Type II (group training activities), and Type III (individual and small group investigations). Type I activities expose students to a variety of topics, occupations, events, and experiences that are typically not a part of the regular curriculum. The purpose of these activities is to expand the scope of experiences for students, stimulate interests that might lead to more intensive projects, and provide teachers with guidance for developing Type II activities.

While Type I enrichment heightens student awareness of special topics, Type II enrichment can best be thought of as "how to" enrichment. Type II activities develop students' abilities to think critically and creatively and teach students skills that help them pursue learning in a topic of interest. Type III enrichment comes into play when a student wishes to pursue more in-depth learning in a particular topic by becoming a first-hand inquirer, investigating a topic as a professional in the real world would. Type III activities cannot be planned in the way many school assignments and activities are planned. Instead students who express a desire to investigate a topic take the lead in identifying real-world problems to address and a real-world audience (not just the teacher). Appendix A provides a more detailed description of Type I, II, and III activities.

Principles of High-end Learning

1. Each learner is unique, and, therefore, all learning experiences must be examined in ways that take into account the abilities, interests, and learning styles of the individual.

2. Learning is more effective when students enjoy what they are doing. Consequently, learning experiences should be constructed and assessed with as much concern for enjoyment as for other goals.

3. Learning is more meaningful and enjoyable when content (i.e., knowledge) and process (i.e., thinking skills, methods of inquiry) are learned within the context of a real and present problem. Therefore, attention should be given to opportunities to personalize student choice in problem selection, the relevance of the problem for individuals and groups who share a common interest in the problem, and strategies for assisting students in personalizing problems they might choose to study.

4. Some formal instruction may be used in high-end learning, but a major goal of this approach is to enhance knowledge and thinking skill acquisition gained through *teacher instruction* with applications of knowledge and skills that result from *student construction* of meaningfulness.

Excerpted from Renzulli, J. S., Gentry, M., and Reis, S. (2003). *Enrichment clusters: A practical plan for real-world, student-driven learning* (p. 8). Mansfield Center, CT: Creative Learning Press.

Figure 1.2. The principles of high-end learning.

In addition, the Enrichment Cluster school structure of SEM provides in-depth, real-world, student-driven learning opportunities to students during the regular school day. Based on the principles of high-end learning (see Figure 1.2 above), students and cluster facilitators come together during the regular school day to explore the methodology of a field and develop an authentic product or service for a real audience. For example, in a cluster on investigative journalism, students might learn research skills, interview techniques, and writing and revising skills to produce an investigative piece that they could submit to the local newspaper or television station.

Administrators from across the nation recognize the value of the enrichment learning and teaching strategies in SEM. These methods help children by providing the necessary opportunities, resources, and encouragement to achieve their potential. Ana's story illustrates the positive impact SEM can have on a young person's school experience.

Engaging a Youngster in the Fabric of School Life

Ana came from a poor village in El Salvador with her mother, father, and three little sisters. Her mother took care of the family in El Salvador and, upon arriving in the U.S., continued to care for the family as they eased their transition to a new country and culture. Ana's father found occasional work as a landscaper, hoping to build a brighter future for his family. Ana spoke little English and, once enrolled in school, spent her time in her new classroom drawing in the margins of her papers. She sketched beautiful fashion designs while her classmates worked on their studies.

Students like Ana, for whom English is a second language, often do not qualify for the enriching educational experiences offered in gifted programs because of the language barrier and cultural differences. But because Ana attended an SEM school, Ana's gifts were not overlooked. The teachers in Ana's school sought to tap Ana's artistic talent and interest in fashion design as a way to engage her in school life. They noted Ana's passion for illustration and took the time to review the interest survey she completed when she entered the school, the same interest survey administered to all students at the school. They knew that nurturing her interests and talent could be one way to engage her. Her teachers met to discuss creative ways to show Ana that her studies and commitment to learning were necessary aspects of becoming a successful fashion designer. They wrote a letter to a famous designer, who responded that she would meet with Ana.

One winter day, the school gathered in excitement as they waited for the limousine that would whisk Ana, her parents, the reading teacher, the enrichment specialist, and Ana's classroom teacher to the fashion designer's studio. It was filled with the work of creating beautiful gowns for celebrities to wear at an upcoming international event. Over the course of the day, Ana learned that there are many things that fashion designers need to know and be able to do to bring their ideas to reality. Designers need to know how to read, write, and do mathematical calculations to create patterns for their clothes. Ana began to see how she needed to apply herself in school in order to pursue her dream of becoming a fashion designer. Ana began to love school and had an outstanding year.

6

2

GIFTED EDUCATION POLICY AND THE SCHOOLWIDE ENRICHMENT MODEL

School boards across the nation have created mission statements emphasizing a vision to meet the individual learning needs of all students. A synthesized version of mission statements found in many school district manuals reads, "All students, including those who are exceptional, are entitled to a public-supported education in which instruction is geared to their needs, interests and developmental level" (Reis, Burns & Renzulli, 1992, p. 3). Although most school boards rely on their administrators to transform the policy statement into a reality, many administrators lack the knowledge and wherewithal to push beyond political barriers and other constraints that hamper progress toward instituting the policy. Successfully implementing SEM depends on how savvy you are about the socio-political and cultural changes of yesterday and today and whether you have a steadfast vision to promote your students' learning, their creative productivity, and the success they are capable of achieving. Examining the trends in gifted education and misguided past decisions will help you understand the passion aroused within the field and respond to the needs and desires of your students, their parents, school staff, and the community.

A Brief History of Gifted Education in the United States

Gifted education in the United States has had a bumpy ride. During the mid-1800s when the United States was an agrarian nation, most communities did not consider the intellectual development of children a priority. They valued knowledge of the basics and the ability to work hard in the field or around the farm. Despite the massive technological and economic changes in our society, the attitudes that reigned in the mid-1800s still exist today as educators "teach to the middle" to make sure all students learn the basics. While wanting to enable all students to achieve on some level is an admirable goal, this practice has left many high-ability youngsters to fend for themselves, offering few opportunities to explore their abilities and realize their true potentials (Gardner, 1983, 1993; Renzulli & Reis, 1985, 1994; Torrance & Sisk, 1997).

In the early 1920s, American society began to realize that there was such a phenomenon as intellectually gifted children and began to think about issues and concerns affecting this population (Terman, 1925, 1959). Unfortunately, by the second half of the twentieth century, addressing the unique learning needs of gifted youngsters was once again placed on the back burner. The political indifference toward gifted education changed only when nations began competing for world power status.

The Cold War era ignited an intense interest in gifted education in the United States. The concern that we would not be able to compete with the Soviet Union and maintain our status as a world power was the motivating force behind this interest. In 1958, Congress passed the National Defense Education Act that made technical assistance and limited funding accessible to states wishing to identify able students and develop programs (O'Connell, 2003, p. 604).

In the late 1960s, public acceptance of the belief that every child has a civil right to a free and appropriate educational program accelerated the development of the field of specialized education. The Gifted and Talented Education Assistance Act of 1969 was the first federal legislation to address this population. Although the act did not mandate that states provide services for these children, it made technical assistance and limited funding accessible to states wishing to develop programs.

In 1972, then Commissioner of Education Sidney P. Marland published a report to Congress on the education of the gifted, concluding that

> School programs for the gifted were hampered in part by apathy and even hostility among administrators; our most valuable natural resource was being neglected; gifted children were in fact deprived and could suffer ill effects of their abilities to function well, which was equal to, or greater than, similar deprivation suffered by any other population with special needs. (p. 24)

In 1977, The Education For All Handicapped Children Act was enacted to protect the educational rights of children with special needs. The needs of gifted children were excluded. This exclusion created a minority population that was "special without special education" (Dodd, 1987, p. 65). Competition for inadequate financial resources (special needs versus the gifted) contributed to the mindset that by providing funding for gifted children, learning disabled children would lose valuable limited funds (Whitmore, 1987). Even though it was up to individual states to ensure that all students' needs were being met (Irvine, 1991), most states had no laws or mandates that regulated gifted programming.

During the 1980s, support for gifted education once again flourished as evidenced by the number of states providing programs for gifted children. Congress passed The Jacob K. Javits Gifted and Talented Students Act of 1988, and in 1990 the National Research Center on the Gifted and Talented was created through federal funding under the Javits Act to provide states with research-based programs and projects. The current federal definition of giftedness is based on the definition in the Javits Act. This definition reflects the influences of Gardner (1983), Renzulli (1978), and Sternberg (1985) on the field of giftedness:

> Children and youth with outstanding talent perform or show the potential for performing at remarkably high levels of accomplishment when compared with others of their age, experience, or environment. These children and youth exhibit high performance capability in intellectual, creative, and/or artistic areas, possess an unusual leadership capacity, or excel in specific academic fields. They require services or activities not ordinarily provided by the schools. Outstanding talents are present in children and youth from all cultural groups, across all economic strata, and in all areas of human endeavor. (The Jacob K. Javits Gifted and Talented Students Act, 1988)

While this federal definition was designed to be adaptable and inclusive and bring services to more students, practices varied across states. Many identification matrices continued to be exclusionary. For example, youngsters who demonstrated performance in only one specific academic area or who were underachievers could be excluded from receiving services. The talents of disadvantaged and minority children were frequently neglected in the early '90s. Almost one quarter of American children were living in poverty (Ross, 1993, p. 5), and these students' talents and gifts often went unrecognized (Ford & Frasier, 1999).

State and federal initiatives directly influenced policy development in gifted education; particularly those centered on funding priorities. During the 1990s a developing apathy, likely influenced by budgetary constraints, once again emerged. Studies conducted in the early 1990s (Purcell, 1993; Beck, 1992) indicated that many gifted students were not being served at all. The U.S. Department of Education's report, "National Excellence: A Case for Developing America's Talent" (Ross, 1993), informed the nation of a "quiet crisis" facing schools:

> The United States is squandering one of its most precious resources, the gifts, talents and high interests of many students. . . . In a broad range of intellectual and artistic endeavors, these youngsters are not challenged to do their best work. The problem is especially severe among economically disadvantaged and minority students, who have access to fewer advanced

educational opportunities and whose talents go unnoticed. (p. 1)

With the publication of this report, meeting the needs of gifted and talented students made headlines and more interest in meeting the learning needs of all students, including the gifted, emerged. Debate raged over how best to accomplish this goal. A variety of recommendations offered in the government report included broadening the definition of giftedness, setting challenging curriculum standards, and increasing learning opportunities for disadvantaged and minority students.

The Gifted and Talented Students Education Act of 1999 continued funding gifted and talented education in the United States. With recent emphasis on high standards and the continued work at the National Research Center on the Gifted and Talented, providing differentiated services for gifted youngsters across the nation has picked up considerable momentum. However, even though the National Association for Gifted Children synthesized research regarding best practices in gifted education and published *Pre-K-Grade 12 Gifted Program Standards* (1998), there still remains a lack of consensus about the most appropriate way to identify and provide programming options for gifted and talented students. Most recently, the No Child Left Behind Act (NCLB) of 2001 has challenged educators by requiring greater specificity in the areas of accountability, assessment, and meeting standards.

Using SEM to Respond to the Educational Needs of Students

Since 1985, hundreds of schools in the U. S. have adopted SEM as a framework for bringing high quality education to all students. Books and articles on the model have been translated into several languages worldwide. More and more administrators have expressed interest in SEM because they see it as a viable way to meet raised public expectations for excellence, demonstrate accountability, and achieve overall school improvement in a flexible, easy-to-implement format. However, there are a fair number of critics of SEM, and it is important to be aware of what both parties have to say.

What SEM Offers

Many researchers and school administrators have found SEM to be an excellent program for providing services to gifted students and for extending those services to meet the needs of students not formally identified as gifted. Given the highly diverse student populations in our schools, coupled with the high-stakes testing movement and cry for accountability, administrators across the country and in countries around the world see SEM as a practical way to engage diverse learners in educational programming that can lead to higher achievement, greater creative productivity, and more enjoyment in school.

In my many interviews with SEM administrators, I discovered a common theme underlying why administrators implemented SEM. Almost uniformly, they believed in their students' potential to achieve. They believed in developing the talents of all their students, not just a select few, and they wanted students to be engaged in learning and enjoy school. Ultimately, these administrators wanted to provide the best education possible to each individual student and saw SEM as the best model available for achieving that goal.

Figure 2.1 outlines why so many administrators today are responding to the needs of their students by implementing SEM.

SEM is a Model for Total School Improvement

Many scholars in the field of gifted education as well as many general educators see SEM as a model capable of leading an entire school toward excellence. The educational structures associated with SEM are infused throughout the instructional program, and, therefore, children identified as gifted as well as their "non-gifted" peers have opportunities to engage in meaningful learning activities (i.e., more students have a chance to investigate real-world problems and present solutions to a real audiences). As Robert Sternberg (1999) states, "Largely through his [Renzulli's] efforts, gifted education has become something more than a story about high-IQ children placed in pull-out classes or special schools" (p. 67). Olszewski-Kubilius concurs: "SEM broadens the range of services for gifted children beyond what is typically found in a gifted program" (1999, p. 56).

Administrators I interviewed chose SEM because it promotes the broad range of advanced-level experiences and higher-order thinking skills referenced in most learning standards and serves as a catalyst for upgrading educational experiences for all students. They encouraged teachers to use the service delivery components

"I hope for a halo effect for my entire student population. The challenge is to use the strategies of SEM to continue to go deeper and inspire all of our students to do better, raising the bar for everyone."

Why Choose the Schoolwide Enrichment Model?

- SEM is a model for total school improvement

- SEM successfully reconciles research and practice

- SEM builds parent/community relationships

- SEM focuses on the optimal development of individuals

- SEM opens the door to an equitable education

- SEM honors cultural diversity

- SEM addresses the underrepresentation of minority students in gifted programs

Figure 2.1. Reasons administrators implement SEM.

"SEM seems to find the hooks to get kids involved. Students who typically trudged through the school day displayed a new energy and excitement about being in school. Their grades improved and so did their attendance."

of the model—the Total Talent Portfolio, curriculum modification techniques and enrichment learning and teaching strategies—not so much because they are tools and strategies for teaching gifted and talented students, but because they can improve overall achievement. Furthermore, because SEM offers opportunities to discover and capitalize on student talents and gifts, SEM administrators believe program activities will get students excited about being in school, and this excitement will translate into more active and engaged learning.

SEM Successfully Reconciles Research and Practice

The practical classroom application of the components of SEM provides high quality experiential learning in line with research studies that indicate that student learning is most successful when (a) new ideas are connected to what students have experienced, (b) students are actively engaged in applying their knowledge to real world problems, (c) learning is organized around clear, high goals; and (d) students can use their own interests and strengths as springboards for learning (Resnick, 1987). Within the defined structures and instructional strategies of SEM, students acquire a sense of their own strengths and talents and have opportunities to use their higher-order thinking skills to pursue learning commensurate with their intellectual ability. These are the very skills students will need when entering the world of work later in their lives.

SEM Builds Parent/Community Relationships

Because "public education is rooted in the political arena" (Tirozzi, 2003, p. 54), many administrators recognize the importance of involving parent groups and business and community organizations in school programs. SEM embraces these groups, bringing them into the fabric of school life though enrichment clusters, mentorships, and other opportunities. By including them in schoolwide enrichment activities, these groups come to better understand and support the effective instructional practices that lead students to higher levels of achievement.

SEM Focuses on the Optimal Development of Individuals

"SEM works for all students to open doors to the enrichment landscape, which continuously is extended and expanded for the extremely gifted. Basically, if a student needs something special, our district usually finds a way to get it."

SEM provides opportunities for students to engage in learning that goes far beyond what a basic general education curriculum provides. Teachers using the strategies of SEM are always on the lookout for students' responses that indicate an interest or ability to pursue more in depth learning experiences. SEM provides the framework that focuses on developing the maximum potential of each student. As Olszewski-Kubilius explains, "The spirit of SEM is to be ever watchful for discerning signs of talent and potential in children within everyday school situations" (1999, p. 56).

SEM Opens the Door to an Equitable Education

In 1992, the American Association of University Women Report "How Schools Shortchange Girls" stimulated great interest in changing educational practices to provide a more equitable education for boys and girls, stating, "Our goal is to ensure equal chances for all public school students to learn, excel and achieve educationally" (p. iv). Opportunities, resources, and outcomes should be available without favor; in other words, "When equity is the goal, all gaps in performance warrant attention. . . . Rather than hold girls to boys' standards, or vice versa, schools need to give students the resources each needs to achieve a universally held high standard" (p. 2). SEM does just that; it helps teachers develop rigorous learning environments for all students based on their individual needs, abilities, and interests.

SEM Honors Cultural Diversity

Many students for whom English is a second language have talents that go unnoticed as they struggle with a new language and culture (Friedman, 2003). Unable to speak English fluently, these children may not be able to qualify for services offered within an existing traditional gifted program. Because SEM encourages educators to look at a complete picture of a student—assessment scores, products, interest inventories, learning styles, etc.—students who do not normally test well because of language or cultural differences are still considered for a range of enrichment experiences.

SEM Addresses the Underrepresentation of Minority Students in Gifted Programs

Growing diversity within school populations has illuminated inequities in access to gifted education programs. The Office for Civil Rights data projections for 1994 indicated that American Indian, Asian/Pacific Islander, Hispanic, and black students are underrepresented in gifted programs as compared to White students. Data in Table 2.1 show participation in gifted programs by ethnic group.

The discrepancy between the percentage of blacks in the student population and the small number admitted to gifted programs constitutes an ethical issue for many educators (Brown, 1997), and the issue of the underrepresentation of Latino and American Indian students identified for gifted programs is difficult to dismiss. Ford (1999) believes that there are four major barriers that contribute to the underrepresentation of black and Hispanic students in gifted programs: "(a) minority students' low performance on standardized tests; (b) low teacher referral rates for minority students; (c) poor communication about gifted education services to minority and low socio-economic status families; and (d) minority students' decisions not to participate in gifted education services" (p. 118). Further-

Table 2.1. Participation by Ethnic Group in Programs for the Gifted and Talented*

Ethnic Group	1980		1994	
	% Served in G/T Programs	% of Total Enrollment	% Served in G/T Programs	% of Total Enrollment
American Indian	0.3	0.8	0.80	1.04
Asian/Pacific Islander	3.8	1.9	5.90	3.72
Hispanic	4.7	8.0	6.25	12.71
Black	9.1	16.1	8.33	16.85
White	82.0	73.3	78.71	65.68
Total	100.0	100.0	100.0	100.00

*From the U.S. Department of Education, Office for Civil Rights, National Summaries of Projected Data, 1980 and 1994 Elementary and Secondary School Civil Rights Compliance Reports.

more, Shade (1994) and Hale-Benson (1986) concluded that black students prefer active, relevant experiential learning opportunities to inactive, irrelevant, and disconnected learning experiences. Ford (1999) agreed: "Black students report being less engaged with pseudo-tasks and disconnected activities and more engaged and motivated with meaningful and real world educational experiences" (p. 120).

The literature shows that SEM has the capacity to reverse "the persistent, pervasive, and unnecessary underrepresentation of minority students in gifted education" (Ford, 1999, p. 118). Because Renzulli's model focuses less on scores and more on interests and motivation, minority students find more opportunities to receive services. In addition, SEM focuses on engaging students in finding and solving real-world problems within an authentic context, providing solutions and outcomes to real-world audiences (not just groups of students and teachers who only happen to be studying the same topic), and this type of learning fits with what Ford reports that black students prefer.

Although implementing SEM can be a way of reducing unequal access to services, it won't be uncommon for you to experience frustration and adverse reactions from your stakeholders if you push too fast. SEM can help you provide equity in educational experiences when coupled with thoughtful analysis into why inequitable conditions exist. In an attempt to create an equitable racial balance, one principal rushed to include ten percent of the minority population in his school's talent pool. Though his intentions were good, he recognized that more work had to be done within the total school program to expose all students to enrichment learning and teaching strategies within the regular curriculum before attempting sweeping changes.

"We found in the last two years that some kids were not ready. [As a result] we have made identification more stringent beginning this year. Emphasis on the schoolwide enrichment strategies of SEM has helped us minimize the predicament of placing students in learning situations for which they were not yet ready."

Anticipating Concerns

Stakeholders happy with traditional gifted programs may have a lot of questions about how a program that offers services to all students will be able to address the needs of identified gifted students. Following are some questions they may have. Keep in mind that much of what has been said against SEM is based on opinion rather than grounded in research. In fact, my interviews with administrators revealed many criticisms did not play out in reality. However, anticipating and considering questions stakeholders might have will help you develop thoughtful responses.

Does Schoolwide Enrichment Dilute Gifted Education?

Some people believe the emphasis on schoolwide enrichment shifts the focus away from properly meeting the needs of gifted children (Jellen, 1985, DeLisle, 2003). Jellen (1985) argued that Renzulli's Enrichment Triad Model (1977) "appears to be nothing but a motivational device that has been aggrandized to theoretical and national status by claiming to offer meaningful educational programming for the gifted" (p. 14). Similarly, Kontos, Carter, Omrod, and Cooney (1983) suggested that "regardless of numbers, to include children in gifted programs whose abilities are less than exceptional is to dilute the effectiveness of intervention strategies designed for exceptional children" (p. 38).

However, administrators I interviewed did not find that SEM diluted gifted education services in their schools. While, pullout programs did address the learning needs of gifted students, it was typically only for short periods of time each week. SEM offered gifted students enrichment learning experiences throughout the school day—that is, whenever they needed it. The fact that SEM offered similar opportunities to "non-identified" students had no effect on the challenge level extended to gifted students.

Does SEM Provide a Defensible Method for Identifying the Gifted?

Jellen (1985) argues that Renzulli's conceptualization of giftedness lacks an "understanding of the major domains and mental qualities of the gifted mind" (p. 14). Pendarvis, Howley, and Howley (1999) noted that SEM requires students to meet three criteria (interest, motivation, and above-average ability) instead of one (IQ) and disagreed that "a child selected for above-average ability, creativity, and task commitment is more likely than unselected children to grow up to perform extraordinary feats in a highly specialized field" (p. 78).

Because this is such a controversial topic, it is important to examine the source and determine whether or not the critics have conducted quality research to back up their allegations. An examination of the writings of Jellen and Pendarvis, Howley, and Howley reveals that their work falls closer to the category of journalistic opinion rather than hard core scientific research; the tone of their comments clearly indicates that they believe giftedness and high IQ are one and the same. This point of view has been largely discredited by leading scholars in the field as reported in *Conceptions of Giftedness* by Sternberg and Davidson (1986). Furthermore, Renzulli's article on The Three Ring Conception of Giftedness (1978) is the most widely cited article in the field, and the identification instruments developed by Renzulli and other researchers (Renzulli, Smith, White, Callahan, & Hartman, 1976; Renzulli, Smith, White, Callahan, Hartman, & Westberg, 1997, 2002; Renzulli, Smith, White, Callahan, Hartman, Westberg, Gavin, Reis, Siegle, & Sytsma 2004) are the most widely used instruments for identification in the world.

The best way to understand how Renzulli recommends identifying students for special services is to review the article "A Practical Plan for Identifying Gifted and Talented Students" in *Scales for Rating the Behavioral Characteristics of Superior Students—Revised Edition: Technical & Administration Manual* (2002). In this article he examines how abilities (including high IQ) are used in combination with other criteria to provide more flexibility in the identification process.

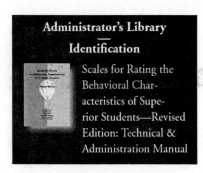

**Administrator's Library
—
Identification**
Scales for Rating the Behavioral Characteristics of Superior Students—Revised Edition: Technical & Administration Manual

Is SEM Difficult to Implement in this Age of Accountability?

Although many in the field see value in the premise underlying the model, Johnsen (1999) has raised concerns about the practicality of implementing the program in this era of school reform, assessments, and accountability:

> The Schoolwide Enrichment Model requires that general education curriculum materials be modified and matched to individual student learning rates and styles. With pressures of increasing diversity and mandated state tests, such a modification is indeed transformational for the majority of schools. While the SEM promises to provide enrichment services to a greater number of students; develop their expertise in a given domain; and build collaboration among students, parents and teachers, and other educators, can all of its organizational and service delivery components be successfully implemented? (p. 111)

Despite challenges to being able to fully implement the model when state and federal testing demands (e.g., the requirements of the No Child Left Behind Act) loomed large, administrators I interviewed did not seem overly concerned. They recognized that the high standards and advanced levels of academic challenge combined with the model's specific strategies for modifying and differentiating the curriculum would help them meet mandates and achievement requirements.

Will There Be Adequate Funding If SEM Replaces Traditional Gifted Programming?

Johnsen (1999) expressed concern that with the focus on developing talents of all students, state mandates and weighted formulas that follow the identification of special populations may be lost. Funding was an issue for all the administrators I interviewed, although none expressed a concern that funding would be eliminated if SEM replaced traditional gifted programming. The specter of inadequate funding actually seemed to mobilize many administrators to seek alternate funding sources. In the search for additional funding, administrators reached out to prime interest groups and community resources, thus creating a greater awareness about SEM and what it can do for students.

A Commitment to Ensure the Best Possible
Educational Program for Students

Few could argue with the volume of research that has been conducted on SEM that continues to this day (see Appendix C for a summary of research on SEM and related models). The experiences of so many administrators worldwide validate the strength of the model as a way to meet the needs of all your students, including your high-ability students.

"I have always felt that if we're going to grow a productive society, to change the future and face the challenges that are ahead, we all have the responsibility to find and nurture whatever it is in children that enables them to be the people we need for tomorrow. And as I looked at all the different models and strategies, I just kept coming back to the fact that there are so many things unknown. So, if we broaden the view and look not only at [developing talent in the] highly gifted, which I also believe in, but if you look at talent development in children who may otherwise be missed, you just might find the next Einstein."

3

Searching for the Best Means of Implementation

As with any new initiative, implementing SEM will present you with a variety of challenges. Conditions and circumstances particular to your school community affect implementation, and implementation will progress in different ways depending on your administrative style. Different approaches to implementing SEM yield three discrete frameworks—Collaborative, Mandated, and Blended—and the type of framework under which you implement SEM is determined by a range of issues, including educational, socio-political, economic, and moral-ethical considerations (see Table 3.1), that have a direct impact on how smoothly the implementation process proceeds. If you are aware of the different frameworks before you begin implementing SEM, you can make more informed decisions about the manner in which you embrace SEM, anticipate reactions to particular issues, avoid common pitfalls, troubleshoot, and plan ahead.

Table 3.1. Issues Affecting Implementation

Educational Issues are comprised of the administrator's ability to infuse the educational structures and organizational and service delivery components of SEM into their total school educational program.

Socio-Political Issues are comprised of the administrator's ability to respond to various stakeholders. How stakeholders view SEM provides the socio-political context in which administrators function.

Economic Issues are comprised of the administrator's ability to secure funding to implement SEM.

Moral-Ethical Issues are comprised of the administrator's moral and ethical commitment to ensure the best possible educational program for all students in their schools.

Three Implementation Frameworks

Collaborative Implementation Framework

Under a Collaborative Implementation Framework (CIF), administrators work with their colleagues to determine if SEM is a good match for their school community. Administrators and their faculty are not forced to implement SEM; rather they select the model because it matches other initiatives in the school and fits with what the faculty envisions for their students. A shared school vision emphasizing a belief in the value of SEM is a defining element of the CIF.

Mandated Implementation Framework

The Mandated Implementation Framework (MIF) is initiated by an administrator in a position to authorize the implementation or by some external pressure on the administrator (e.g., central office, school board, U. S. Department of Education Office for Civil Rights). Those mandating SEM make the decision to implement with little input from colleagues. Frequently implementation is rushed and various stakeholders have little time to internalize the philosophy of SEM, making acceptance of the model and successful implementation more challenging.

Blended Implementation Framework

The Blended Implementation Framework (BIF) includes elements of both the CIF and MIF. A governing body or decision-maker exerts pressure to broaden gifted education services to more students and suggests SEM as a match between school and community needs. For example, school leaders in a district under government watch due to concerns that minorities are being discriminated against in the district's gifted program might recommend SEM as a way to offer services to more gifted minority students. If the district chooses to implement SEM, it is with input from the faculty. The directive to change schoolwide practices is balanced with thoughtful, conservative movement toward implementing a model that seems right for the school. Under the BIF, administrators bring information about SEM to colleagues and express a preference for SEM as the model of choice, but they consider input from faculty as part of the implementation process.

Table 3.2 depicts some of the distinguishing qualities of each framework.

Influences on the Implementation and Success of SEM

None of the three frameworks provides a fail-safe approach for implementing SEM. What might be an ideal framework for you and your school might not be possible for another administrator. Each implementation framework carries with

Table 3.2. Distinguishing Qualities of Implementation Frameworks

Framework	Characteristics	Facilitating Conditions of Framework	Constraining Conditions of Framework
Collaborative Implementation Framework (CIF)	Belief in the value of SEM Stakeholders deem SEM a good match to school community	Can ensure faculty buy-in is loaded on front end of SEM implementation	May require proactive behaviors to gain adequate funding
Mandated Implementation Framework (MIF)	Pressure exerted to implement SEM as a means of broadening services	Clout that comes from an officially mandated program Availability of funds	Possible resistance to implementation because stakeholders were not a part of decision to implement Tendency to rush implementation to satisfy directive
Blended Implementation Framework (BIF)	After a mandate, collaboration with staff results in determination that SEM is a good match to school	Clout that comes from a mandate to "do something" Can collaborate with stakeholders to steer away from conflict	May feel pressure to rush implementation to satisfy directive

it certain dynamics and influences to consider. Following is a discussion of these influences and how they can affect implementation. Chapters 4-7 detail practical strategies to help you make the implementation process successful.

Teacher Buy-in

Various forces pulling in all directions (multiple educational initiatives, union and contract limitations, public expectations, the standards movement, etc.) influence teacher buy-in. And because SEM presents a different approach to learning and teaching than more traditional methods, bringing the theory behind SEM into educational practice can be a challenge to some teachers.

Concerns about getting teachers to buy into the educational strategies of SEM are common across all three implementation frameworks. However if you function within the CIF or the BIF, chances are you will be able to obtain buy-in before implementation and, thus, minimize negative reactions. No matter which framework you are working under, take the time to examine what your teachers are already offering in their classrooms and extra-curricular programs and point

"We looked at what we already had in place and what we believed in. Where are we currently? What is the profile of our students? And which of these models works with what we have?"

out the similarities between their current classroom activities and SEM. For example, if your teachers are organizing interest-based groups after school then they are already in a mode where the identification and the growth of the students' talents are valued.

If you select SEM with the support of at least 75% of your staff, you will experience less resistance than if you forge ahead without staff consensus. Even with 75% of your teachers willing to implement, you still need to bring a sizeable proportion of teachers into the program. SEM will require some teachers to re-conceptualize their approach to instruction, and you must be prepared to ease the transition so that they do not feel they are being asked to do something additional or threatening. Even the most user-friendly, respected models can quickly become history if teachers perceive a lack of administrative support.

Operating within the MIF typically results in a larger group of teachers unwilling to undertake SEM. If you take the view that you have to fix your school and make your colleagues modify their teaching, you may find that teachers have a harder time adjusting. Mandating SEM and moving forward without engaging in professional conversations and adequate staff development activities can incite the anger and reluctance of some staff who may then try to undermine the implementation process. However, even if you must work within the MIF, you can take steps to encourage teacher support and buy-in. For example, if you emphasize the general principles, encourage teachers to examine what they are already offering their students, take their suggestions on how best to implement SEM, and develop a viable plan with their input, they can become more open to the philosophy of the model. Thoughtful leadership, no matter the framework, is critical to success. Chapter 5 examines the issues of teacher buy-in in greater detail.

Vocal Parents

When implementing SEM, you can expect to hear from vocal and influential parents. There will always be parents who support SEM and parents who oppose it, especially if they aren't made aware of the positive impact SEM can have on their children's education. Parents who do not have complete information about the model are often worried that their gifted children will not be challenged within SEM's enrichment format as compared to a traditional gifted pullout program. Additionally, many parents feel a sense of pride that their youngster "made it into the gifted program" and may not want to support a program that is more inclusive.

You can enhance the climate surrounding implementation by educating parent groups about how SEM offers students a broad range of advanced-level learning experiences that develop the higher-order thinking skills outlined in your local learning standards. As a CIF or BIF administrator, you can convey the benefits of the model by involving parents in the collaborative decision-making process. Criticism and verbal attacks give way to more receptive attitudes when parents feel that they have a hand in decisions regarding SEM activities for their child. Administrators implementing within the MIF seem less able to successfully advocate for SEM because they spend much of their time defending decisions they make in isolation. Chapter 6 focuses on understanding the needs and the wants of parents and your community.

Accountability

School boards may direct central office administrators to account for the way they provide gifted education services to students. Sometimes external pressure, perhaps the Office for Civil Rights, mandates that a school system implement a model that provides access to services to more students without specifying the model. The administrator then becomes accountable for choosing the program. This kind of pressure is a powerful political force and you must make every attempt to come to grips with it early.

Faced with accountability issues, a school board mandate for SEM can be beneficial. You can keep zealous parents and teachers at bay by referring to the board resolution and declaring that you are following the recommendations of the approved program. It is amazing how much clout an official document can impart.

In lieu of a mandate, CIF and BIF administrators can refer to a Professional Development Plan. Chapter 4 addresses the importance of creating a Professional Development Plan.

Access to Funding

As with any program, the availability of funding can affect your SEM program. Types of funding sources and the amount of money available to implement SEM vary from locale to locale. Generally, you can tap three different sources for funding: (a) state and district funding, (b) fundraising initiatives, and (c) grants.

Funding is one area in which having a mandate for SEM can be a strong asset. Typically a mandated district program is accompanied by funds to meet the mandate. If you function within the BIF or MIF, you would likely fall into this category. If you are in a CIF framework, you still may be able to convince your central administration that the program represents the collected vision of the staff and/or parents and therefore providing adequate funding would be seen as an acknowledgement of the district's respect for your school's move toward implementing the enrichment learning and teaching practices that everyone wants.

Many states provide funds for students who are identified as gifted (typically the top 3%-5% of students based on nationally normed achievement test scores and/or group or individual IQ tests). Some states also allow districts to identify students based on multiple criteria, including parent and teacher referrals, but these students may not be included in the state count for funds unless specific state criteria for giftedness are met. While this funding issue may be a stumbling block for some, for others, it may actually be liberating. You may find that you have greater freedom in making choices you strongly believe in without the constraints that often accompany traditional funding sources.

Chapter 7 looks at various ways to tap funds for your SEM program.

4

THE PROFESSIONAL DEVELOPMENT PLAN AND TIMELINE FOR IMPLEMENTATION

Though you can begin infusing enrichment learning and teaching strategies into your existing program almost immediately, it is important to structure a plan with attainable goals and methods for monitoring progress. This plan, the SEM Professional Development Plan (PDP), should incorporate a solid understanding of your school's needs, capabilities, and desires (where you are now) and outline explicit goals (where you want to be). The following list of questions, by no means exhaustive, will help you begin to think about elements you should include in your PDP:

1. Does your district have specific professional development plan requirements that you should follow?

2. Does your district provide a template that would help you develop your plan? (If not, ENC Online provides an abundance of information, resources, materials, and planning tools that can help you develop your PDP (www.enc.org/pdguide).)

3. What do you think are the components of an effective professional development plan?

4. Specifically, what do you hope to accomplish by implementing SEM?

5. What strategies or activities will help accomplish those goals?

6. How will you involve your stakeholders?

7. How will you evaluate the plan's effectiveness and monitor progress?

8. What physical evidence will you be able to show to students, staff, parents, and the community that the SEM program is accomplishing your goals?

The SEM PDP should address overall philosophy, instructional strategies, professional development, parental involvement, and technical assistance to support the plan and include three phases of implementation: (a) gathering a Schoolwide Enrichment Planning Team, (b) introducing the strategies of SEM, and (c) refining application in your school. These three phases of implementation are the core of the PDP.

An SEM PDP typically spans a three- to five-year timeframe and details year-by-year and often month-by-month implementation goals. The Conclusion in *The Schoolwide Enrichment Model: A How To Guide For Educational Excellence* (Renzulli & Reis, 1997) details recommendations for a five-year plan and should be read and thought of as a guide before moving on to the three phases of implementation.

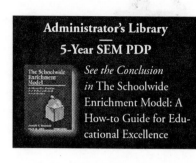

Administrator's Library
5-Year SEM PDP

See the Conclusion in The Schoolwide Enrichment Model: A How-to Guide for Educational Excellence

Phase 1: Gathering a Team and Defining Its Purpose

The Schoolwide Enrichment Planning Team is responsible for a wide variety of tasks. They develop the Professional Development Plan, review and recommend enrichment resources, and determine how best to use resources in the general educational program. The Schoolwide Enrichment Planning Team generally consists of the principal, the enrichment specialist, three or four classroom teachers, parents, and when appropriate, a student, although other combinations of educators and community resource people are possible. Many school districts also hire a Schoolwide Enrichment Model Program Facilitator to serve as a guiding hand behind the SEM Planning Team. Appendix B includes a job announcement for such a position.

This team structure may already be in place in your school. Many school systems have a mandate from their state to organize a site-based decision-making team that plans and implements various school initiatives. In some schools, principals struggle with the direction the Site-based Decision-making Team takes and suggesting the team take on schoolwide enrichment is typically met with enthusiastic approval because of the positive impact it can have on everyone involved. Many principals have told me that having the Site-based Decision-making Team function as the Schoolwide Enrichment Planning Team has been very helpful. However, be aware that using the Site-based Decision-making Team as the SEM Planning Team only works if SEM is the sole agenda.

"Our 1st year our SEM team was not as effective perhaps because we attached this committee to our Site-based Decision-making Team. We found that most of our time at meetings went to managing other issues rather than SEM. Now our SEM operates independently of the Site-based Decision-making Team. The SEM team is singularly focused and able to do more. Our enrichment specialist serves on both teams to keep communication open."

If you do not already have a team in place, invite volunteers to join you. Organize an awareness session in which you introduce the model, the research behind it, and how SEM has the capacity to improve teaching practices and student achievements throughout the school while meeting state and federal requirements.

The team, whether it is comprised of volunteers or functions as the Site-based Decision-making Team, should administer interest inventories to all students. The data they gather from the inventories will help them plan schoolwide and

---

The Fuller School

To: Members of the Site-based Decision-making Team
From: Dr. Grant, Principal
Re: Student Interest Inventories

As we determined at the end of last year, this year's team initiative will be to promote talent development in our students. The first order of business for the professional staff will be to administer the interest inventory *If I Ran the School* to all students in grades 2-8. The teachers are putting the finishing touches on a pictorial version for children in grades K-1. I anticipate that the inventories will be administered and collected prior to our next scheduled meeting. Since I was chosen to facilitate that meeting, I am going to bring all of the inventories for tallying by grade level and by school. Three parents, Mrs. Fried, Mrs. Gallo, and Mrs. Hawkins, will complete the tallying off site if we do not finish the task at this meeting. Mrs. Gallo has graciously volunteered to graph the results of the students' interest areas on a large poster that we will place on display in the front corridor of the building. I would like to add to the next meeting agenda a discussion of the types of activities that we want to offer students based on the results of these inventories.

Figure 4.1. Sample memorandum to site-based decision-making team.

classroom enrichment opportunities. Figure 4.1 presents a sample memorandum that you can use when you and your team are ready to tally the inventories.

Scheduling mentors, speakers, and performances that are designed to augment the scope of enrichment for all students in the school is also a part of the Planning Team's responsibility. The team should first look at the entire school staff for potential speakers. One principal was ecstatic to find an accomplished flutist and a Shakespeare buff on her staff; both were more than willing to share their talents with students. Offering "Inspiration" (Renzulli, Gentry & Reis, 2003), an adult interest survey, to interested staff members will help them examine their own experiences and talents. Don't forget to analyze your community's businesses and services. (You can modify "Inspiration" to use with members of the community.) Ask business owners if they or any of their employees would be willing to share their expertise with students. Figure 4.2 lists the steps for developing a resource databank of volunteers.

The Schoolwide Enrichment Planning Team should also provide professional development activities as well as present enrichment learning and teaching techniques to their peers. Chapter 6 in *The Schoolwide Enrichment Model* describes the curriculum compacting process and provides professional development training activities. Additional information about curriculum compacting can also be found in *Curriculum Compacting* (Reis, Burns & Renzulli, 1992) and *It's About Time* (Starko, 1986).

A vital part of the team's work is to demonstrate the connection between SEM and state learning standards. As administrator, it is important to work with the team to compare the language associated with SEM with the language in state learning standards and draw out the similarities. Showing how SEM

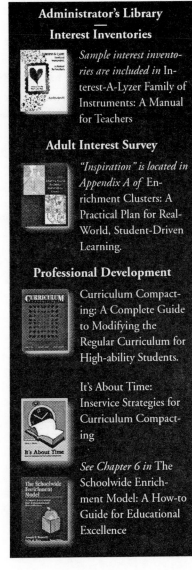

Administrator's Library
—
Interest Inventories

Sample interest inventories are included in Interest-A-Lyzer Family of Instruments: A Manual for Teachers

Adult Interest Survey

"Inspiration" is located in Appendix A of Enrichment Clusters: A Practical Plan for Real-World, Student-Driven Learning.

Professional Development

Curriculum Compacting: A Complete Guide to Modifying the Regular Curriculum for High-ability Students.

It's About Time: Inservice Strategies for Curriculum Compacting

See Chapter 6 in The Schoolwide Enrichment Model: A How-to Guide for Educational Excellence

---

Developing a Resource Databank

1. Survey the entire school to identify people who are willing to share their expertise with students.
2. Analyze community strengths:

Town Government	Town Departments
Chamber of Commerce	Educational Facilities
Social Agencies	Health Care Facilities
Private Businesses	Industries
Seniors	Parents

3. Contact members of the community through surveys, direct calls, or personal contact.
   - Use public service announcements, news releases, and feature articles to inform the public of your desire to involve them in school activities.
   - Send letters to universities, colleges, etc. asking for any volunteers who would be willing to share their passions with students.
   - Send surveys home with students or include them in school newsletters or brochures to help identify parents who would be interested in volunteering.
4. Encourage parents, teachers and students to locate resources.
5. Respect the rights of volunteers regarding publicity and willingness to share their expertise. Make sure potential volunteers are aware that you are collecting information about talents to keep on hand for teachers who might want to ask them to give a lecture, facilitate a discussion, lead an enrichment cluster, be a mentor, etc.
6. Gather information on volunteers in a resource bank on directory cards or in a computer database.
7. Make sure school staff know where to find the resource bank and how to contact speakers for their classroom.

Adapted from information found in Renzulli, J. S., & Reis, S.M. (1985). *The schoolwide enrichment model: A comprehensive plan for educational excellence* (pp. 256-259). Mansfield Center, CT: Creative Learning Press.

Figure 4.2. Steps for recruiting resource persons.

activities satisfy and exceed the standards will improve teacher buy-in and parent and community acceptance. Consider the following example comparing New York State Learning Standards in social studies to skills developed in an Enrichment Cluster.

In an Enrichment Cluster on historical events and immigration, students and the facilitator examined the history of immigration into the U. S. through Ellis Island from a variety of perspectives: through the eyes of immigrants, workers in Ellis Island, and others alive at the time. Activities helped students learn how to analyze both primary and secondary resources. Students also learned interview skills in order to gather oral histories. To share the information they gathered, cluster participants decided to create a living museum, stressing the significance of items that have been passed from generation to generation through the last 100 years. In this cluster, participants met the following New York State learning standard: "Students will use a variety of intellectual skills to demonstrate their understanding of major ideas, eras, themes, developments, and turning points in the history of the United States and New York."

Use this example with your faculty to show how SEM activities meet state standards. You can arrange a grade level or faculty meeting where members of the Schoolwide Enrichment Planning Team can demonstrate the alignment between SEM activities and your state standards. The Schoolwide Enrichment Planning Team can win many parents over by emphasizing that students participating in SEM activities are acquiring the intellectual skills expected in state learning standards.

Generating a Timeline for Implementation

As mentioned earlier, the Schoolwide Enrichment Planning Team is responsible for developing a PDP that charts implementation activities. Phased-in procedures will nurture the infusion of SEM's high-end learning strategies into your total school program, and infusion is the key word! The best way to sabotage SEM is to rush its implementation. Built into every good SEM PDP is a realistic timeline. A timeline helps you keep track of steps you have taken and steps you still need to take as you move through the process of implementation. Timelines can span one year or cover a two- or three-year timeframe. Figure 4.3 presents a comprehensive three-year timeline that details both district office and school activities for implementing SEM components and strategies and other district initiatives. You can design a simpler timeline as long as it contains the critical components to get the job done. The template in Figure 4.4 can help you organize activities. If you develop a timeline that covers a longer period of time, you should establish regularly scheduled review periods to reassess goals and time frames.

Phase 2: Introducing Strategies of SEM

During Phase 2 of implementation, the Schoolwide Enrichment Planning Team introduces specific instructional strategies. Although SEM has clearly defined structures and components, you must first emphasize the components that best match your own school. Many schools first introduce enrichment clusters because they are appealing to teachers, do not require a lot of funding, are a source of great excitement for students, and can get parents and the community involved. Other administrators have chosen to introduce a few interested teachers to curriculum compacting. As these teachers gain experience with this differentiation management technique, they can then serve as mentors to other teachers learning how to use curriculum compacting.

As you progress with implementation, you will want to communicate what

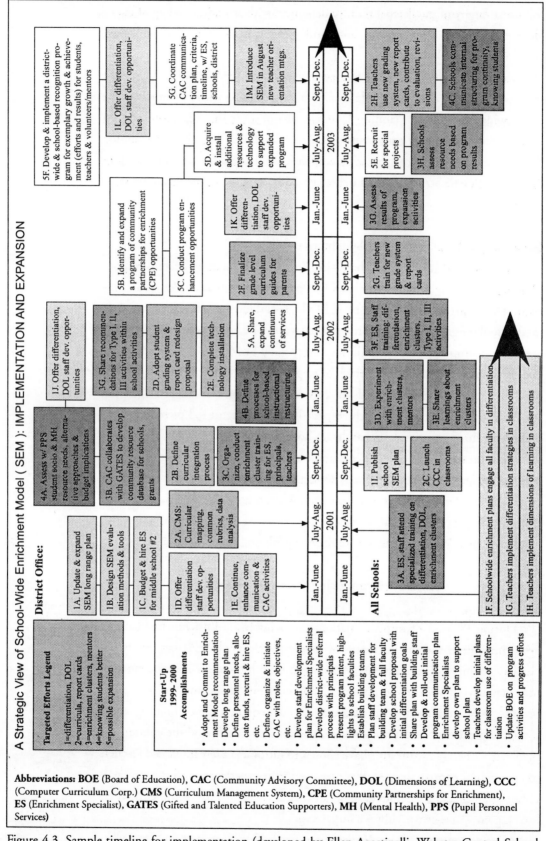

Figure 4.3. Sample timeline for implementation (developed by Ellen Agostinelli, Webster Central School District, Webster, NY). Used with permission.

Timeline for Implementing a Schoolwide Enrichment Model Program

Overall Program Goal:

Goal:

Activity(ies)	Responsible Party(ies)	Timeline	Documentation of Accomplishments	Completion Dates Targeted	Actual

Goal:

Activity(ies)	Responsible Party(ies)	Timeline	Documentation of Accomplishments	Completion Dates Targeted	Actual

Goal:

Activity(ies)	Responsible Party(ies)	Timeline	Documentation of Accomplishments	Completion Dates Targeted	Actual

Figure 4.4. Template for creating a timeline for implementation.

is going on in your school to parents and the community. Ellen Agostinelli of Webster Schools developed a progress report for parents (see Appendix B) that described the status of the SEM program, how it affected students, and specific steps the district would be taking to continue to develop and improve the program. Agostinelli used this report to do more than tell parents about the program; she used it to encourage parents to become involved in their child's enrichment. It invites parents to contact their child's teacher, enrichment specialist, and principal with questions or concerns and encourages them to bring enrichment home—to involve children in extra-curricular activities and unstructured play, to model a curious approach to the world, and to plan side trips to historical landmarks, museums, and workshops during vacations. Just as Agostinelli has done, make sure your communications with parents present a two way street: provide information and encourage responses. Parents are more likely to support a program and a school that they feel they understand and that engages them in active involvement.

Phase 3: Refining Application in Your School

An SEM program is always a work in progress as it responds to the continually changing student body, staff, and wider community as well as periodic reviews of the program. The final stage of implementation involves assessing program effectiveness and refining components of the model.

Working in this era of greater accountability, gathering and reviewing data about student performance will help you report necessary information to the public as well as help your staff make adjustments in their teaching methods. Request regularly scheduled articulation meetings during which grade level teachers meet with teachers feeding students into and following their grade (grade two teachers meet with grade one teachers and grade three teachers and so on) to discuss patterns of success and areas needing improvement. During one articulation meeting held in my school, the testing coordinator and teachers in grades three and four reviewed the item analysis for recently administered English language arts and mathematics assessments. As a group, they poured over the information in search of areas of competence and areas of weakness. They easily identified where the instruction was solid and where additional emphasis was warranted. Because these articulation meetings were held on a regular basis, the group also examined strengths and weaknesses of groups of students over time. This information helped us develop plans to revise our instructional programs and form flexible learning groups to address areas of strength and weakness. Due to my staff's efforts, my school was recognized by the state as one of the most improved schools over a three year period, with test scores soaring in all areas.

In addition, allow your teachers opportunities to discuss their creative teaching methods—what works and what doesn't. Encourage them to share their ideas and the results of their efforts. If some teachers have figured out a way to successfully compact students in mathematics, arrange time for other teachers to visit with colleagues' classrooms to observe them in action. Give them time to debrief the experience. When they begin to see their students working harder and smarter on materials better suited to their needs, they will realize their teaching methods are becoming more effective.

Parents and members of the community can also offer valuable insight into the progress and status of your SEM program. It is important to forge strong relationships with the wider school community and encourage them to offer feedback on the program. Inviting parents to become involved in the program from the outset demonstrates your desire to hear and respond to their input. However, you may also wish to conduct regular meetings during which you invite parents to voice concerns, ask questions, or even respond to surveys on the program. (See Chapter 6 for more information on communicating with parents.)

Finally, do what you can to interact with others involved in SEM programs. Attend Confratute, a summer institute on enrichment learning and teaching at the University of Connecticut, or visit other schools implementing SEM and take opportunities to exchange ideas, experiences, and lessons learned. Staying in touch with other SEM administrators can help you maintain a vision for your program. (Chapter 8 lists web sites that can help you get in touch with other SEM schools.)

Thoughtful, planned implementation will help you and your staff develop a school environment recognized for encouraging the full development of the learner instead of seeing a student as a repository for information to be assessed with the next round of standardized tests.

Your role in preparing your students for the future is more important than ever before. It is in your best interest to work with your colleagues to devise a PDP that functions as a beacon of light focused on bringing out the best in your students and their teachers.

5

STRATEGIES FOR ACHIEVING
TEACHER BUY-IN

In public education, many teachers are tired of feeling inadequate and rushed as the perception that their work has to be "fixed" prevails in the community and in the media. With enormous pressure to "get the scores up," it should be no surprise that some teachers initially see SEM as one more program viewed through rose-tinted glasses by administrators long out of the classroom. Don't be discouraged; you can demonstrate the benefits of SEM and gain more support by providing the resources, professional development, and, most importantly, time for teachers to become comfortable with SEM.

Making Implementation a Collaborative Process

Collaboratively developing a professional development plan for SEM will reduce much of the reluctance teachers feel. Allowing teachers to have input into the implementation process offers them ownership and some control over the program. In addition, finding ways to align implementation activities with other ongoing initiatives facing your teachers serves to protect and preserve one of their most valuable resources—time. If teachers see how SEM strategies fit in with their current classroom and schoolwide initiatives, they will feel less like it is an added burden on their very tight schedule. By easing in professional development activities, communicating with staff about the model, and not expecting too much too soon, most teachers will make a positive adjustment to SEM. If you respond to teachers' enthusiasm and concerns, they will feel included in the process of implementation and begin to view the enrichment learning and teaching strategies associated with SEM as a way of meeting the needs of all students, including the high-ability students in their classrooms. How quickly you can bring enrichment

"I think that the curriculum compacting service delivery component is appealing, but I'm not sure they're ready for that this year. I think the best place to begin is with enrichment clusters because teachers can buy-in."

learning and teaching strategies to students depends on your faculty's readiness to implement.

Engaging Staff in Discussion

Begin preparing teachers for SEM by engaging them in self-reflection activities. We have all been students at one time or another, yet how often do we talk about our own school experiences and the people who influenced us? Activity A provides you with a format to begin conversations. This activity will help you establish a positive tone of sharing and listening in your building, helping teachers become more receptive to the introduction of SEM.

Activity A: Leaving a Lasting Legacy

PURPOSE:	**To discuss influences on career paths**
TIME:	**20-30 minutes**
SETTING:	**Participants at tables**
MATERIALS:	**Paper, markers, overhead projector or flip chart**
DESIGNATION:	**Essential**

This activity engages participants in sharing and self-reflection. The knowledge you gain about your staff through this activity will help you explain to your staff how SEM will support them in fulfilling what they hope to be as educators.

Divide participants into small groups and ask everyone to share with their colleagues why they became educators and who may have influenced their decision to enter the profession. Do they have the passion to pass on the legacy to others? Ask them to think back to the gifts they received from a mentor/educator and then think forward to the gifts that they can bring to a child. Though this activity may seem very simplistic, the reasons participants chose to become educators are incredibly varied, and the discussion can remind participants of the influence those who may have inspired them had. Have volunteers share their stories to the larger group and call attention to any trends.

Activity B builds on the conversations begun in Activity A, asking teachers to discuss what they think a "good education" is.

Activity B: Professional Promenade

PURPOSE:	**To discuss what makes a good school**
TIME:	**20-30 minutes**
SETTING:	**Weather permitting, somewhere outside**
MATERIALS:	**Paper, markers, overhead projector or flip chart, clipboard for participants (one per group), *Fish! Sticks* video (optional)**
DESIGNATION:	**Essential**

This activity engages participants in self-reflection and discussion. Before organizing participants into small groups, initiate a discussion on what learning and teaching should be. To inspire this type of discussion, you may wish to have participants view a video entitled *Fish! Sticks*. This amusing video describes how a sleepy little fish market in Seattle became world famous when employees developed a vision. (See Appendix D for more information on this video.)

On a flip chart or overhead projector list one or two beliefs about teaching, learning, and good schools (e.g., there are many ways to be smart, there are many ways to group students for instruction, etc.). Divide participants into small groups and ask them to share with each other what they envision for students in their school: What do they believe translates into an excellent education? What should the school environment look like? Ask participants to take a clipboard and marker and, as a group, move to a spot on the school campus to discuss their beliefs. Encouraging groups to go outside moves them to a more relaxed environment where some participants may feel more comfortable sharing their thoughts. If the weather is bad, participants can either stay where they are or move to another room in the building. Ask a volunteer in each group to record the group's beliefs. Return to the meeting room and have each group recorder present his or her list to the larger group. List responses on a large chart or overhead projector titled "At [insert name of school] We Believe . . ." This discussion helps set the stage for aligning beliefs with actual practices by showing how SEM matches what they say makes a good school.

Note: You may want to turn the final list into a large poster to place on display in a heavily trafficked area of the school (e.g., a main hallway). The poster could include a "Photo Gallery" of students/staff engaged in the activities on the list. The teachers in my school believe in interest-based learning so we display photographs of students participating in enrichment clusters and Type I activities.

Activity A encouraged your staff to share best practices in teaching and learning from their own experiences and Activity B had them explore what they believe is good teaching. Using the Compacting Readiness Checklist (Starko, 1986) in Activity C will prompt teachers to think about the disparity between what they say they believe their students deserve from a quality education and what they actually deliver.

Activity C: Classroom Practices

PURPOSE:	**To examine whether current classroom practices are aligned with beliefs about good teaching**
TIME:	**Approximately 10 minutes**
SETTING:	**Participants take checklist home, then return for general discussion session**
MATERIALS:	**Compacting Readiness Checklist (see Appendix C) and pencil**
DESIGNATION:	**Optional**

Prior to the session, distribute the Compacting Readiness Checklist (Starko, 1986) (included in Appendix C). Ask participants to complete the checklist and bring it to a discussion session scheduled within a few days of distribution. Make sure participants know that you will not collect the checklists. Explain how to interpret the results: If there is an approximate 1:1 ratio between Part A and Part B, then there is a good alignment between a teacher's beliefs and his or her classroom practices. If their is a discrepancy between Part A and Part B (Part A yields a much higher number than Part B), then the results are more like the many teachers who have a difficult time making their beliefs come alive in the classroom setting.

The checklist is a tool to help the participants identify discrepancies between their personal beliefs about good teaching and their classroom practices. The checklist opens the door to understanding the many factors that can cause practices to diverge from beliefs (e.g., mandates, standardized testing, too many educational initiatives, etc.). At the discussion session, ask participants why they think teaching practices might differ from beliefs about what makes good teaching. Participants can speak in general terms or talk specifically about their own experience. Explain that further discussions in other activities will focus on ways that SEM helps teachers recapture the excitement and creativity they hope for in their teaching.

Note: Some administrators encourage participants to leave anonymous notes in the facilitator's mailbox during the week following distribution of the checklist. The facilitator can then address the anonymous comments in the group discussion.

These three activities will set the stage for stimulating teachers' interest in SEM. Most likely, the model is philosophically aligned with the very same learning and teaching practices that they enthusiastically spoke about in Activities A and B. Table 5.1 presents the links between typical teacher beliefs and SEM. Once you are aware of your teacher beliefs, you and your team can scour your SEM library of resources and make your own SEM connection.

Sparking and sustaining interest in educational initiatives can sometimes be a challenge. One way to engage staff is to locate a brief article that you feel will provide readers with useful information about SEM. Avoid articles that are lengthy or contain a lot of theoretical information unless that is your express purpose. (You can find a variety of articles on the web site for the Neag Center for Gifted Education and Talent Development at www.gifted.uconn.edu.) Post a copy of the article in an area frequented by staff along with a sticky note stating, "Colleagues, if you are interested in this article, please sign below and a copy will be placed in your mailbox." Make a copy of the title page of the article with the sticky note listing the names of staff who requested the article and place it in a "tickler file" for one week later. During the week, seek out colleagues who requested a copy and engage them in an informal conversation about the article. After a week or so passes, in-

Table 5.1. Teacher Beliefs and the SEM Connection

Teacher Beliefs	SEM Practices
There are many ways to be smart.	SEM identifies interests to help students develop their strengths.
Learning should go beyond the acquisition of basic skills.	SEM promotes high-end learning, talent development, leadership and creative productivity.
All teachers can learn.	SEM fosters the continuous, reflective growth-oriented professionalism of school personnel.
Learning can be fun.	Challenging enrichment experiences replace routine desk work.
All students must have the opportunity to develop their unique abilities.	High level learning opportunities are available to all students in the school.
Learning should be relevant and meaningful.	Students apply relevant knowledge, research, creative, and critical thinking skills to the solution of real problems.
Flexibly grouping students for instruction should be a priority.	Grouping practices vary as curricular adjustments are made to match students' learning needs.
School should be a focus on the positive.	SEM capitalizes on enriching students rather than "fixing" them.

vite those who requested the article to join you for coffee and "sweet treats" and to share thoughts about the article.

Activity D is another format that can get everyone thinking and talking more about SEM.

Activity D: From Paper to Reality

PURPOSE:	**Relating SEM on paper to classroom realities**
TIME:	**45-60 minutes**
SETTING:	**Small groups of six to eight arranged in a circle**
MATERIALS:	**Multiple copies of an article or excerpt from a book about SEM, highlighters, marker, index cards, pens or pencils**
DESIGNATION:	**Essential**

This activity can solidify participants' connections with each other and their understandings about SEM and its various components. Participants will discuss how the model matches what they said they believe in and value for their students. The activity can be conducted in a variety of settings, including faculty meeting, grade level meeting, etc.

Distribute a short article or book excerpt on SEM at the beginning of the session. Ask participants to silently read the text and select one statement from the article that they feel "says it all." Ask the participants to record the statement on an index card and note where the statement is (page #, paragraph #). When everyone is finished, break up into small groups. Ask for a volunteer in each group to begin by reading the statement he or she chose. Each person in the discussion group (except the reader) then responds to the statement. For example, one participant might choose the statement, "Enjoyment and interest can be the very ember to ignite a true love of learning" and another might offer the following response: "I can recall a tremendous burst of interest from a little boy in my class whenever we spoke about airplanes. He knew everything about how they worked, what they were made of, and all about their designs. I saw a spark in him that I don't typically see, and I was impressed with his wealth of knowledge. This sentence that you selected made me think of him." Participants do not have to contribute a response to each statement read. After everyone has a chance to react, the reader gets "the final word," elaborating on why he or she selected the excerpt. The process continues until everyone has read his or her statement.

Note: If time is limited you may wish to provide the article and materials prior to the session. In a memorandum, provide the directions to read the article, underline or highlight text that evokes meaning, and note where the text is. Explain that at the faculty meeting everyone will be organized into small groups to react to the text.

Moving Forward

How will you know when the time is ripe to begin? A high level of teacher buy-in is desirable to move forward. As with any new initiative, if less than 75% of faculty is willing to begin the implementation process, you may face a host of barriers and resistance. Continue to work to create a shared vision with your staff. The following process can be helpful: Suppose Table 5.1 (on page 39) was the list of beliefs your teachers generated. Select one item from the list as an area of concentration and plan a faculty meeting that focuses on that area. For example, you might choose "learning should be meaningful and relevant." Invite teachers to the faculty meeting to celebrate the ways they make learning meaningful and relevant in their classrooms. Give them time to prepare (two weeks should be ample time), asking them to bring samples of student work, teacher generated materials, lesson plans, or anecdotes to share that demonstrate that this type of learning is occurring in their classrooms. During the faculty meeting, break teachers up into small discussion groups and encourage volunteers to share what they have brought.

How you break teachers up into groups is an important consideration. You can group teachers randomly, but you run the risk of having too many of the reluctant teachers in the same group. You can group teachers by grade levels with special area teachers (music, art, etc.) assigned to each group or you can group them across grade levels (K-5, 6-8, etc.). This final grouping arrangement provides teachers with a schoolwide view of this type of learning. No matter how you group teachers, your goal is to disperse the reluctant teachers among groups of more positive teachers.

Over several months continue selecting different beliefs from your list and planning faculty meetings that are forums for sharing successes. Continue having formal and informal discussions with teachers, sparking interest with pertinent articles, and engaging teachers in additional Activity D sessions. This approach will help teachers recognize the connection between their beliefs about quality education and SEM and raise the percentage of teachers willing to implement.

As the school leader, you must show sensitivity to the challenge some of your staff members will face. SEM requires a philosophical shift from traditional methods of teaching, moving away from viewing students through a remediation lens to the spectrum of enrichment. Introduce Activity E to widen the doors of discussion. When you take the time to listen, your staff will appreciate your support and

"I'm a big believer in shared vision. I don't think you can move anywhere without it . . . We really worked hard on the shared vision around some of the philosophical things we believe in, and so it [SEM] came from us."

commitment, and you will be in a better position to work through the challenges together.

Activity E: Facing Challenges

PURPOSE:	**To address possible challenges to implementation**
TIME:	**10-15 minutes**
SETTING:	**Participants at tables**
MATERIALS:	**Paper, markers, overhead projector or flip chart**
DESIGNATION:	**Essential**

Divide participants into small groups. Ask each group to brainstorm challenges that they may face during implementation. Some typical responses are funding, time, and staff development. The list below presents a sample list of challenges generated by a group of educators who participated in this activity. Generally, the lists of challenges are consistent from school to school. Don't be surprised if your teachers generate a similar list.

Challenges

- identifying link between SEM/assessments/accountability/district mandates/curriculum
- getting parents involved
- taking what teachers do and expanding upon it
- scheduling
- getting true commitment
- finding the time
- minimizing teacher reluctance/resistance
- adapting model to the school
- funding
- finding best way to approach professional development
- evaluation

Invite each group to share their top three challenges with the whole group, instructing participants to avoid repeating any challenge already shared. Record challenges on chart paper or transparency for future reference. Assure participants that as you progress through the implementation process, each challenge will be addressed and checked off the list. Within a day or two of the meeting provide each participant with the list of challenges and ask them to think about how they can overcome them.

Set a tone that moves teachers from focusing on the challenges alone to "How can we do this?" Tell them to meet as a grade level and generate at least three ways to conquer some of the challenges on the list. It's best if you don't participate in this meeting. After each grade level has met (don't forget your special area teachers), arrange another faculty meeting with the agenda "Overcoming Challenges." Once again, organize teachers into discussion groups to talk about their solutions. Be sure to generate a list of their suggestions that everyone can refer to as the school moves through the implementation process. This brief activity can help reduce the anxiety teachers feel whenever a shift in teaching practices occur. It demonstrates your commitment to listen to them throughout the implementation process.

This next case study provides an excellent example of how a principal's approach to introducing SEM can help teachers and staff feel more comfortable with the program.

The Power of Professional Conversation

In a small suburban elementary school located in the Northeast, Mr. McMallalue, the newly assigned principal, grappled with the thought that the current trend of standards-based, high-stakes testing could limit the talent development of students in his school. After much thought, he decided that developing the gifts of his students must become a focal point of the school. He knew that he had to take time to understand the values of the community, the current state of affairs in the field of education, as well as the beliefs his colleagues held regarding teaching and learning before he could orchestrate any significant change.

First he decided to learn as much as he could from his colleagues about what had brought them to the profession of education. He organized a series of professional conversations that took place in many different forums (faculty meetings, grade level meetings, informal breakfasts, and the all-important discussions in the hallways), looking for connections between what teachers believed and their current practice. Having served in another school as an enrichment specialist, Mr. McMallalue was aware of SEM and wanted to use the model to facilitate enrichment learning and teaching strategies to benefit his school's increasingly diverse populations. He decided to take his time introducing SEM and demonstrate to his staff how the model matched what they said they believed about quality learn-

ing and teaching. After several weeks, he, along with faculty, staff, and parents, designed a course of action that matched what they all hoped their school could be.

With his slow and steady support, the teachers eventually felt comfortable enough to distribute and analyze student interest surveys. The interest survey became a document symbolic of their belief in the value of interest-based learning. Over time issues associated with long-term implementation became less contentious. Together, with the assistance of the Schoolwide Enrichment Team, they examined SEM from a professional development perspective and determined the kind of support and resources the teachers needed to implement successfully. Designing professional development initiatives sensitive to the paradigm shift associated with enrichment teaching and learning helped ease his colleagues into this new view.

Mr. McMallalue believed that collaborating with colleagues to focus on student interests and strengths would engage students in learning, foster motivation and improve achievement. Talking with his colleagues about why they became educators, what they valued, and how they managed their classrooms helped him identify specific aspects of SEM already in practice or that were in line with what teachers had said they believed in. Mr. McMallalue encouraged teachers to infuse aspects of SEM throughout the school by connecting SEM to these values. Teachers began to use SEM practices not because Mr. McMallalue directed them to, but because they saw how it fit with their desire to develop an engaging, challenging, and exciting learning environment for all of their students.

As you increase support for SEM and establish a vision grounded in the principles of enrichment learning and teaching, you can begin designing a suitable program consistent with your school's needs and resources. But before forging ahead, you must contemplate how to infuse SEM into your existing school schedule while respecting the teachers' contract.

Working With the Teachers Union

Like most administrators, you want a productive relationship with the teachers union. Union activists may attempt to block aspects of SEM that they perceive as "pushing the envelope" of the teacher contract. If, for example, you do not develop an appropriate schedule for enrichment clusters (or Academies of Inquiry) with teacher input, they may think that they will lose valuable, dedicated preparation time to make room for the programming changes. Protecting the integrity of preparation time is vital, and modifying the SEM implementation plan by allowing teachers to opt out of offering an enrichment cluster if the schedule impacts their preparation time shows teachers you are aware of their concerns and willing to make modifications. See Figure 5.1 for a sample memorandum that a concerned principal might send to members of his staff to minimize any resistance.

An effective way to minimize confrontations with the teachers union is to maintain a good relationship with your staff. Be aware of your management style and its effect on your staff. If you put yourself on a pedestal and present yourself as the "last word" in all discussions, your teachers may approach the union first when they have concerns about the program. If, on the other hand, you invite teachers to open discussions during which they feel that their comments will be respected and acted upon, they may not feel a need to go to the union. Likewise, respect your faculty's collective power and know each of your teacher's limitations and strengths. The more you know about your staff the better able you will be to anticipate their concerns, allowing you to address them before they even raise them.

Scheduling

If you find yourself compromising what's best for your students because of constraints in your schedule, then it's time to take a creative look at the scheduling method. Once you feel confident that most of teachers want to begin, you or, better yet, your Schoolwide Enrichment Planning Team can suggest reducing existing periods by five minutes to create a new block of time for enrichment activities. Administrators tell me that this plan works well in a tight schedule. Some schedule

"*People went to the union and said I was taking their preparation time, which was never true. So, at the end of the year, I explained that organizationally we were not ready to do Academies. Representatives from the union called me and explained that they really wanted to run the Academies with modifications. So I created a shortened schedule, and they still said no. They claimed their preparation time was still encumbered and they weren't willing to do that.*

"*One teacher summed it up best for me when he said, 'We trust you but we don't know who the next administrator will be. If we give the fifteen minutes of preparation time here and thirty minutes more student contact time, and this administrator comes in and doesn't want to do SEM, the precedent has been set and the preparation time is lost forever.' That made the most sense to me. And so I compromised. If the Academy runs during a teacher's prep time, then the teacher doesn't have to do one. We'll get more community people to participate.*"

Granger Middle School

To: Judie Foster, Jim Cummings, Ryan Harper
From: Mr. Lane, Principal
Re: Response to Your Concerns

In response to concerns you raised after the last grade level meeting, I want to assure you that I am not trying to tell you what to teach your students. Instead, I hope that through SEM methods you will develop your own vision of how best to tap the many talents your students have within them.

So that I can better understand your concerns about SEM, please meet with me on Tuesday at 8:30 a.m. I am anxious to hear what you have to share and would like the opportunity to respond to all of your questions and concerns. We are only at the beginning of the implementation, and you have my word that you will have my utmost support. I know that most of us did not learn in our pre-service education how to meet the needs of higher ability youngsters. However, I do see it as our obligation to educate ourselves about what we can do to ensure that all of our students are exposed to optimum learning experiences during their time here at Granger Middle School.

Figure 5.1. Memorandum to concerned teachers.

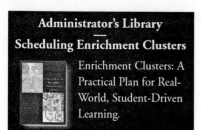

Administrator's Library
—
Scheduling Enrichment Clusters

Enrichment Clusters: A Practical Plan for Real-World, Student-Driven Learning.

a time slot once a week that can be used for enrichment activities, special presentations, and events. Across grade levels, you can isolate protected time (no students leave the room during this designated time), opening up time to offer SEM enrichment experiences or enrichment clusters. My school already had club meetings during the lunch/recess period, I chose to help club advisors tweak how they ran the clubs, rename them, and turn them into enrichment clusters. *Enrichment Clusters* (Renzulli, Gentry & Reis, pp. 36-37) provides information about scheduling. Whenever you are working with the schedule, though, it helps to involve teachers and staff as they are more likely to support changes when they have been a part of the decision-making process.

Familiarizing Teachers with Components of the Program

Keep in mind that most teachers, particularly your more experienced staff members, did not learn how to meet the learning needs of high-ability youngsters during their pre-service education. It is your job to introduce them to new teaching methods. One of the best ways to familiarize teachers with SEM methods is to take them through a simulation. A simulation helps teachers put theory into practice in a risk-free environment, and you can design a simulation for almost any component of SEM. Activity F is a simulation for the enrichment cluster program. After you take your staff through the simulation, Activity G will help elicit your teachers' reactions to the simulation.

Activity F: Enrichment Cluster Simulation

PURPOSE:	**To introduce enrichment clusters**
TIME:	**Approximately one hour**
SETTING:	**Large room**
MATERIALS:	**Chart paper and display easel, colored markers, tacks or masking tape, Comparison Sheet, Sample Enrichment Cluster Sheet, Cluster Simulation Worksheet (one per group) (see Appendix C), and a pencil**
DESIGNATION:	**ESSENTIAL**

The purpose of this professional development activity is to introduce participants to enrichment clusters and establish the difference between clusters and mini-courses. Review the fundamental differences between enrichment clusters and mini-courses (see Comparison Sheet in Appendix C). Using the large chart on display, talk the assembled group through a sample simulation (see Sample Enrichment Cluster Sheet in Appendix C). Ask the group to call out an interest area that adults may be drawn to. (Remind them to keep it clean!) As each person offers an interest area (e.g., wine tasting, cooking, travel, fitness, etc.), record it on chart paper and give it to the person who becomes the "holder" of the interest area. Ask that person to stand somewhere in the room and continue until there are enough interest area selections to break the larger group into smaller groups. Ask the participants to choose an interest area that they wish to develop into a cluster and to stand with the "holder" of the interest area. (For this simulation, participants need not be truly intrigued by the interest area.) Provide each group with a Cluster Simulation Worksheet (see Appendix C), a colored marker, and a pencil and encourage them to relocate to a comfortable area to work. Give them 20-30 minutes to respond to the seven items on the worksheet and record their answers on chart paper. Ask each group to select a spokesperson who will display the completed chart and share it with the larger group. Leave approximately five minutes for each spokesperson to share. End the session by encouraging participants to think about their experience. The next activity requires them to share what worked in the simulation and what challenges need to be addressed to ensure success.

Note: Between professional development sessions, provide articles about enrichment clusters to interested parties (see Appendix D).

Activity G: Comfort and Concerns with Enrichment Clusters

PURPOSE: **To share thoughts about enrichment clusters**

TIME: **Approximately 45 minutes**

SETTING: **General discussion area**

MATERIALS: **Chart paper, marker**

DESIGNATION: **Essential**

After engaging participants in the Enrichment Cluster Simulation, set a date to come together to discuss participants' experiences in the simulation. Begin by asking the assembled group to think about how enrichment clusters align with their beliefs and with what they value for their students. You can begin the process by listing some of your own "comfort starters" (e.g., working with colleagues, interest-based learning, exposing students to real-world work ethics, etc.) Break into smaller groups, making sure that each group includes some "positive" teachers. Ask them to continue to list comforts and then shift to concerns. Ask participants to share their top concerns with the whole group, instructing them to listen carefully and avoid repeating any concern that has already been raised. Record all comforts and concerns on chart paper. As the workshop ends, tell participants that you will provide them with their own list and, at a future meeting, address all concerns. I recommend following the same post-activity procedure described after Activity E ("Facing Challenges").

Note: This activity can be modified to address any component of SEM.

Celebrating Successes

One sure way to encourage teachers is to recognize them for their efforts, however small. Be on the lookout for any opportunity to say, "Good work!" One appreciated gesture is to leave a complimentary note on a teacher's desk after you have visited the classroom: "I am so impressed with the flexible grouping arrangements that you organized for your students. Clearly, the opportunity to work with peers who demonstrate similar learning strengths brings out the best in them!"

When you notice that teachers are using enrichment learning and teaching strategies arrange a Celebration of Talent Development faculty meeting to celebrate successes. Invite teachers from different grade levels and disciplines to mingle with each other and share what is working. Activity H provides a forum for acknowledging the high-end learning going on in your school.

Activity H: Developing a Checklist for High-end Learning

PURPOSE:	**To enhance professional reflection and examine actual samples of student work**
TIME:	**Ongoing**
SETTING:	**Any location where teachers can comfortably meet**
MATERIALS:	**Samples of student work**
DESIGNATION:	**Optional**

Ask teachers to get together with other teachers on their grade level to examine samples of student work that they believe exemplifies high-end learning. Each teacher should bring three samples. Encourage them to discuss criteria for high-end learning. Some questions you can pose to spark their conversation may be: Does the sample represent a superior response to the task? How do you judge what a superior response would be? Is the sample representative of the standards or curriculum objectives expected in your state?

Have teachers sort the samples into three piles: Good, Better, and Best. Teachers should first concentrate on the Best pile and pin down a list of attributes apparent in this group. Write a description of each of the attributes. Then working backwards, have teachers take another look at the

Good pile and judge what a good response would be. Finally, follow the same process for the Better pile. This process ensures that the Best pile truly stands above the rest. Teachers should design a checklist with no more than ten items to help them assess the presence or absence of the attributes in the Best pile. The more checks a sample has, the closer it is to being a high-end learning sample of student work.

Checklists can be designed for all types of SEM related activities: oral presentations, cooperative learning projects, independent study projects, and any discipline-related product developed by the student, etc. In my school checklists are also used for self-assessment and peer feedback. The checklist in Figure 5.2 for high-end learning criteria was inspired by examining mastery level expectations stated in standards and curriculum objectives as well as suggestions from teachers with whom I have worked.

High-end Learning Checklist

__ Work reflects essential information.

__ Main concept easily identified.

__ Content is logically arranged.

__ Spelling and grammar are accurate.

__ Communication is clear, organized, and detailed.

__ Problem solving strategies are identified and applied.

__ Work shows student's ability to draw inferences.

__ Writing purpose is clear.

__ Student applies and transfers knowledge to new situations.

__ Student looks at knowledge from multiple perspectives.

__ Project completed on time or ahead of schedule.

__ Organization enhanced the quality of the product.

__ Student went above and beyond to gather information.

__ Student used multiple resources and methodologies to research information.

__ Work was creatively presented.

__ Student held audience interest throughout presentation.

Figure 5.2. Sample high-end learning checklist

Activity I: Celebrating Student Work That Exemplifies High-end Learning

PURPOSE:	**To celebrate high-end learning**
TIME:	**45-60 minutes**
SETTING:	**Any space conducive for sharing examples of student work**
MATERIALS:	**Sample(s) of student work**
DESIGNATION:	**Essential**

This is a two-session activity. During the first meeting encourage participants to think about how they incorporate high-end learning into their instructional programs. Participants then brainstorm a list of examples and think about student work that reflects high-end learning.

The second session is a celebration of the wonderful high-end learning taking place in your school. Organize participants into small groups that include representatives from each grade level plus special area teachers. Encourage, but do not require, teachers to bring a sample of student work that exemplifies high-end learning to share. After the celebration, you can collect the samples of student work to place in a binder for reference or proudly display them on a bulletin board in the school.

6

COMMUNICATING WITH PARENTS AND THE COMMUNITY

Parents are a vital part of the implementation process and the SEM program. Parents can fill a wide variety of roles in the program, including serving on the Schoolwide Enrichment Planning Team and as facilitators or aides in an enrichment cluster or Academy program. Therefore, just as you need to achieve a significant level of teacher buy-in before implementing SEM, it is equally important to ensure parent and community buy-in as well. Some administrators struggle with how to connect with parents, but building a relationship with parents before trying to get them involved in particular programs is an important step. Over the years, administrators implementing the model have gained faculty and parental consensus on a small number of easy-to-understand SEM concepts and services by providing resources and information related to each aspect of SEM without the educational jargon that befuddles non-educators. The following case study is a good example of how one principal set about connecting with parents.

Building Bonds with Parents

Mrs. Flanagan is the principal of an elementary school located in an impoverished urban area where many parents felt disconnected from the school. To begin strengthening relationships between the parents and school personnel, she asked the school psychologist and a community based social worker to help her develop strategies to bring more parents to school functions and important school meetings. Mrs. Flanagan arranged social gatherings with baby-sitting services and transportation for parents who would not otherwise be able to attend the events. As the bond between the school and parents strengthened, parents began to show interest in participating in

SEM activities. Mrs. Flanagan then organized an awareness session about SEM and described the many ways that parents could become involved.

General Sources of Parent Concern

Regardless of the educational program offered to students, parents will have questions. In response to an SEM initiative, parent comments might be, "What are you doing educationally that my bright child can be a part of?" "How do you intend to support his fast pace of learning?" "Why can't you keep things the way they are?" "My child loves being part of the gifted program, and she'll be dragged down if you include students who won't be able to keep up with her." For many parents, concern about SEM comes from fear of the unknown, as SEM is a dramatic shift from traditional programming models. Others may be reacting to the loss of status they enjoy when they can say that their child has been identified for a traditional gifted program. It is important to assure parents that your school will continue to meet the needs of their high-ability youngsters. Underscore how SEM dramatically expands the amount of time that their child will be exposed to challenging learning experiences. Figure 6.1 illustrates how little time pull-out programs typically serve gifted students.

The parent community needs to understand that adopting SEM does not

"I think parents understood where we were coming from, what we were trying to do. And what I think they want to know is that their child's needs are going to be met."

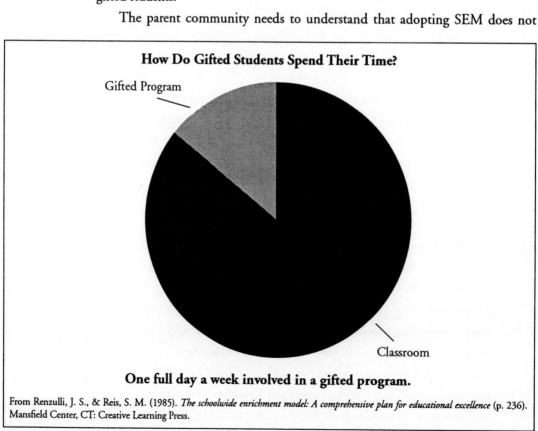

How Do Gifted Students Spend Their Time?

Gifted Program

Classroom

One full day a week involved in a gifted program.

From Renzulli, J. S., & Reis, S. M. (1985). *The schoolwide enrichment model: A comprehensive plan for educational excellence* (p. 236). Mansfield Center, CT: Creative Learning Press.

Figure 6.1. How much time a pull-out program typically serves gifted students.

mean that gifted education services will be discontinued. Rather, the traditional gifted programs that parents are more familiar with will be subsumed within SEM's continuum of services. The goal is to help parents transition from the comfort they feel with the teaching methods of their youth to SEM's broader reach. Find any means possible to communicate that SEM is not taking anything away from their child's education; it is simply enhancing other children's educational experiences by broadening access to what has been traditionally reserved for a select few. To educate parents about SEM, you can transform Chapter 1 into an SEM Awareness Session for parents and invite parents to a "Dessert with the Principal" (see Figure 6.2). Before the evening begins, be sure you have thought about possible parent concerns so that you can respond to them with confidence.

In order to help you prepare for dealing with parental issues, Activity J provides you with insights into potential reactions to SEM. Once you are aware of these feelings, you will be in a stronger position to advocate for SEM effectively.

THE MANNING SCHOOL **PTA** PRESENTS

DESSERT WITH THE PRINCIPAL

JOIN US FOR AN ENGAGING PRESENTATION
ON SCHOOLWIDE ENRICHMENT

PRESENTER:
MRS. JOANN LUSTIG,
MANNING'S ENRICHMENT SPECIALIST

MRS. LUSTIG WILL PROVIDE AN INFORMATIVE OVERVIEW
OF ENRICHMENT IN OUR SCHOOL.

December 2ND @ 7:15PM in the All Purpose Room
Desserts will be served compliments of the PTA.

- -

I will attend: _____
Name(s)

Phone #: _____

Please respond by November 24th

Figure 6.2. Invitation to a PTA presentation on SEM.

Activity J: Point/Counterpoint

PURPOSE:	**To prepare for potential reactions from stakeholders when introducing SEM**
TIME:	**Approximately 30 minutes**
SETTING:	**General discussion area**
MATERIALS:	**Paper, markers, overhead projector or flip chart, clipboard for participants (one per group)**
DESIGNATION:	**Optional**

You can use this activity as a self-reflection tool for yourself alone or with other administrators, the SEM Team, or any group responsible for implementing SEM. The purpose is to understand possible reactions to SEM.

Divide the group in half and ask them to move to opposite ends of the room. Assign one group the role of agreeing with a statement, and the other group will argue against the statement. Explain to them that for the purposes of the activity, they need not personally agree with the argument they will be asked to make. On an overhead projector or flip chart, write the phrase that they will react to: "Providing services for gifted children only is elitist." Allow each group 15 minutes to list their arguments, then record them on the chart. Mix up the group by pairing members of each group together to discuss how to use the arguments to foster implementation.

Use the following list as a reference.

Agree: Providing services for gifted children only *is elitist* because . . .

- they reduce resources for others; funds are disproportionately allocated.
- they lower regular classroom expectations.
- teachers/parents/identified students look down on "regular" students.
- they lower the self-esteem of students who are not identified.
- they widen the gap between "haves" and "have-nots."
- average students miss out.
- they are divisive.
- they become a special privilege.
- they drain the talent pool.
- they foster negative socialization issues.

Disagree: Providing services for gifted children only *is not elitist* because . . .

- they promote excellence in education.
- they match students' specific learning needs.
- they respond to parent/community concerns (keep parents happy).
- they focus resources on gifted children's needs.
- other students become classroom leaders/rise to the top (because gifted children are out of the classroom).
- they challenge students ready to be challenged.
- our society needs to develop the potentials of gifted students.
- they provide comfort for students already perceived as different in some way.
- they can reduce underachievement.

Just as some parents will criticize the program because it casts a wider net, parents with children who might never have been identified as gifted become enthusiastic supporters, happy that their children have the opportunity to participate in enrichment learning and teaching activities. These parents may want to push the program too fast, and you must emphasize to them that their children are benefiting at every stage of implementation.

Parents may also resist SEM because they think that enrichment is replacing basic skill learning. They may not believe that through enrichment, their children will acquire the basic skills associated with the drill and practice of test-prep materials. The parents on your planning team and those who have volunteered as cluster facilitators can help. Encourage them to speak out in support of SEM, explaining how components of SEM (e.g., enrichment clusters) reinforce basic skills and meet state learning standards.

As administrator, it is your responsibility to understand the roots of resistance, whether it's from teachers or parents. The following case study is a fine example of a principal coming to grips with parental resistance and what he needed to do to contain and eventually dispel it.

Combating Skeptics

Mr. Jones, the principal of a large urban middle school in the Midwest, was thrilled to be invited back for his second year. He had worked hard to get to know his school community and he felt confident that he knew what the stakeholders valued for the children in his school. On his flight back from Confratute, the summer institute he attended at the University of Connecticut to learn about

SEM, Mr. Jones fleshed out drafts of a memorandum to send to his staff and a letter to parents explaining the new program he wished to implement in the upcoming year. He was excited to introduce the model with an Academy program, the middle school application of enrichment clusters, in his school sometime within the first semester.

The Teachers

On the first day of school, Mr. Jones readied the room for the first faculty meeting of the year. He provided breakfast treats and allowed ample time for his staff to catch up with each other since they were last together in June. Mr. Jones lowered the lights and enthusiastically began his presentation about SEM and the Academy Program. Mr. Jones stopped from time to time and asked for questions and comments. He was surprised and dismayed when he overheard one of his veteran teachers, Mr. Wilson, whispers to a colleague, "I'm not doing this. We have too many programs already." Other staff members sitting nearby nodded their heads in agreement. Mr. Wilson continued, "We are probably going to lose our current preparation periods since there isn't any time in our schedule!" The union representative stood up and said, "Mr. Jones, we agree that this program sounds terrific. However, given the demands of the state testing program and all of the programs we are already accountable for, we worry that we won't be able to meet our professional obligations if we also have to implement SEM."

The Parents

At the PTA meeting, Mr. Jones prepared himself to answer questions that he anticipated would be posed by parents. Based on his informal conversations with parents during the first few weeks of school, Mr. Jones knew there were some strong feelings about spending school time on anything other than boosting basic skills and preparing students for state assessments. Mrs. Bluster, an extremely vocal parent, searched for any forum that she could find to promote an anti-enrichment campaign. She engaged other parents in conversations at the bus stop and even wrote letters to the editor of the local newspaper reproaching Mr. Jones and the district for allowing the program to exist and displace valuable time for test preparation.

Mr. Jones went home each evening discouraged by the two vocal naysayers who seemed to dog his every attempt to promote SEM. He

was upset that other teachers and parents were not as vocal in their
support as Mr. Wilson and Mrs. Bluster were in their opposition.

The Solution

Reflecting on the situation, Mr. Jones soon realized that he
held some responsibility for the current state of affairs. In his en-
thusiasm for SEM, Mr. Jones didn't take the time up front to have
professional conversations with his colleagues to prepare them to
consider SEM. He did not talk with them about how well SEM
fit with other initiatives already in place in the school. He had
no idea what his colleagues thought about good teaching, and he
didn't explain how SEM activities would propel the students to-
ward higher achievement.

Likewise, parents had no idea that time spent in the Academy
program reinforced the three Rs as well as emphasized skills well
beyond basic competencies. Mr. Jones began to make presentations
to the PTA highlighting the wide array of skills infused into all
SEM experiences and more explicitly made the connection between
enrichment activities and state learning standards. He began to
promote SEM activities in the media, and soon after, the PTA
voted to make SEM activities and programming a line item in
their upcoming budget.

Gathering Data to Find Out What Your Parents Really Think

Finding out what parents think about SEM is an important step. The more
you know, the more likely you are to remove roadblocks that some very vocal
parents may generate. Furthermore, do not take what one parent has to say as
representative of a broad base of parents. While everything that any parent tells
you is important, find out if, in fact, when they say they're speaking for many
that they really are. Many years ago in a former school district, I had a vocal parent publicly state that it was mind-boggling to her that an enrichment program
was displacing instructional time in core subjects. She gave the impression that
she spoke on behalf of most parents. Concerned, I asked the Schoolwide Enrichment Planning Team to administer the survey "Parent Attitudes About Enrichment Opportunities" (Renzulli, Gentry & Reis, 2003, p. 106). The results
of the survey showed that this parent was actually a minority of one! Armed
with the data, I requested permission to present the results at a PTA meeting.
My presentation put an end to the misinformation and perception that parents
did not support the program. Don't be surprised if you discover that "the overwhelming number of parents who agree with me" just isn't reflected in the data.

Administrator's Library
—
Data-Gathering Surveys

See Appendices A and D
in Enrichment Clusters:
A Practical Plan for Real-
World, Student-Driven
Learning.

Enrichment Clusters (Renzulli, Gentry & Reis, 2003) contains other surveys to help you gather data from teachers and students as well as enrichment cluster facilitators.

Encourage parents to contact the parent members of your Schoolwide Enrichment Planning Team with any questions or comments about SEM. Always respond to any questions that a parent might have and offer to meet to discuss concerns. Figure 6.3 presents a letter written to a concerned parent.

Looking at Your School with a Parent's Eye

One way to help parents understand what SEM is all about is to make sure your school visibly reflects SEM. On any given day after classes have begun, take a walk around your school. What do you see? Is there any evidence that your school is a place that values rigorous learning? How would a parent visiting your building know that your school does? Look at your bulletin boards, samples of student work, and descriptions of programs and activities. Is there any evidence that students engaged in SEM activities are developing the higher level of skills expected by your community? Activity K will help you collect and display work that demonstrates that your school is a place where enjoyable and solid learning is taking place.

Ryder Elementary School

January 24, 2004

Mrs. Nancy McNoughton:

During public comments at last night's PTA meeting, you voiced concern that the students who participate in the gifted pull-out program each week will no longer have their learning needs met. I do understand that this type of programming seems to be quite a departure from what you have been used to in the past. Clearly, you had many more questions than time allowed. I would welcome the opportunity to meet with you at your earliest convenience and continue the dialogue before you come to any final conclusions about the program. Every parent's concerns are important to me, and I do hope that you will take me up on this offer. Please contact Mrs. Cromwell at 555-1234 to let her know when you might be available to meet.

Sincerely yours,

Dr. Joseph Kelly
Principal
JK/pc

Figure 6.3. Letter to a concerned parent.

Activity K: Developing Artifacts

PURPOSE: **To find and display evidence of SEM in your school**

TIME: **Approximately 30-45 minutes**

SETTING: **Participants at tables**

MATERIALS: **8½" X 11" writing paper, 18" x 24" construction paper, pencils, markers, thumb tacks or masking tape, Artifact Siting Form (optional, see Appendix C)**

DESIGNATION: **Essential**

If you are just starting implementation, ask participants to think about examples that would show that SEM is working in their school (press releases, letters to parents, bulletin board display, etc.). Provide some time for participants to share their perceptions and then explain that for the next 20 minutes, they will work with a partner to create at least one artifact that could be used to promote SEM.

If implementation is already underway, ask participants to work with a partner to discuss whether or not they feel that there are examples in your building that the enrichment learning and teaching practices associated with SEM are taking place. They should then locate evidence that SEM is at work in their school.

Ask participants to affix the artifacts (either created or genuine) to the wall around the perimeter of the room. Reorganize participants into small groups, with one group in front of each artifact. After several minutes, allow groups to rotate and view the next artifact. (Arranging the viewing time in this way will allow everyone to see each artifact in a timely manner.) Bring participants back together to discuss the artifacts. What makes some artifacts better examples and good promoters of SEM?

In closing, encourage participants to examine their workspace to determine if SEM products and learning experiences are evident. Remind them that visible proof that the school promotes high-end learning can affect public perceptions. An Artifact Siting Form (see Appendix C) can help you keep track of the artifacts in your building.

Publicizing Your Program

Publicizing the SEM activities going on in your school serves two purposes: it demonstrates your accomplishments to the public while generating pride among your students and stakeholders. There are three ways to publicize school events beyond the school-based activities mentioned above: press releases, public service announcements (PSAs), and non-media publicity campaigns. Whenever you are trying to attract attention from the media, be it TV, print, or radio, be sure that the spokesperson can be reached easily. If you select students to speak, be sure to choose students who aren't camera shy and are articulate and well informed about the SEM activity you are promoting. You may need to take time to coach them, as some may be nervous about being in the spotlight!

Press Releases

A press release is a document written to draw media attention at a specific time. Encourage staff to tell you about any specific SEM events that may be news-worthy so that you can pass the information on to the media. Every school district has different policies for dealing with the media. In some schools, the responsibility to promote school events rests with the building administrator. And in other schools, a district liaison deals with the public. Make sure you know and follow your district's policy.

When writing a press release, look for a compelling angle. Connecting your press release to a community-wide event, such as a holiday celebration, can make it more newsworthy. Present the basic facts of your news item, but be creative. A lively quote that elaborates on the basic facts can be an attention grabber. The sample press release in Figure 6.4 will give you a good idea of how to promote enrichment clusters (you can modify it for any of the SEM components). Make sure that the contact person listed on the form can be easily reached (even after school hours) and is a good spokesperson for the event.

Public Service Announcements (PSAs)

A public service announcement is a short radio or television announcement, usually ranging from 10 to 60 seconds, that communicates a special program or event (see Figure 6.5). TV and radio outlets are usually eager to accommodate schools and provide free airtime. When you contact local stations, ask for the name of the person who handles school announcements and how far in advance the PSA must be submitted. Don't be discouraged if your announcement is pushed aside to clear the airways for a significant local, national or international news item. Be persistent and eventually you will be heard.

Non-media Publicity

You can also organize a publicity campaign without the media. You can plan and publicize a Talent Night or SEM Fair. Students can design flyers for the event and leave them in local coffee shops, post them on bulletin boards in the community, or give them to the Chamber of Commerce to distribute. It's even fun to work with the local supermarket and decorate paper grocery bags promoting the event.

Public School 17: The Lowell School
2 Laurel Avenue
Anytown, USA
Phone: 555-8321 Fax: 555-8642
Email: Lowell@internet.com
Principal: Dr. Herman Casey
Assistant Principal: Dr. Regina Reynolds

PRESS RELEASE
FOR IMMEDIATE RELEASE

Contact Person: Ms. Ellen Gold, Enrichment Specialist

BORED CHILDREN DON'T LEARN!

Enjoyment and interest are the buzzwords that you hear as you walk through the halls of The Lowell School in Anytown, USA. Whether you speak with a teacher, a student, or a visiting parent, the message is the same. The Lowell School makes learning fun! The interest inventories administered to each student in this Schoolwide Enrichment Model school showed that the students just loved everything to do with the mysteries of math, science and inventions! Teachers and parents then worked together to make learning challenging and fun by organizing a Bright Ideas Invention Convention for students and community members. By opening up the convention to community members, everyone had the opportunity to appreciate the talents and creative projects produced. Whether young or old, adult or child, the sentiment was the same, "You'll never be bored at The Lowell School!"

###

Figure 6.4. Sample press release.

PUBLIC SERVICE ANNOUNCEMENT

DATE TO AIR:	May 10th, 2004
CONTACT:	Jerri Leopold, Enrichment Specialist
	Warrington Elementary School
PHONE:	555-3322 (daytime); 555-4673 (evening)
EMAIL:	jerri@internetaddress.com
FAX:	555-7860

Spotlighting Student Talents at Warrington

Did you know that the flames of enthusiasm for learning are aglow at Warrington Elementary? Parents and teachers working together with students have organized a showcase of creative student projects. Join the excitement and visit the school's Enrichment Fair set up for the community to enjoy all this week in the All Purpose Room in Warrington Elementary's main building during school hours.

END

Figure 6.5. Sample public service announcement.

As you begin publicizing your SEM program, it is important to learn how to communicate with the press effectively. Activity L can help you and your staff hone your skills.

Activity L: Public Relations Simulation

PURPOSE:	**To prepare for interview situations**
TIME:	**Approximately 45 minutes**
SETTING:	**Large room**
MATERIALS:	**Interview Simulation Sheets (see Appendix C), recording equipment (optional)**
DESIGNATION:	**Optional**

This simulation is designed to help educators learn how to be cautious when dealing with the press. Introduce this activity by explaining to participants that they will role-play an interview situation. Participants will either be an administrator responsible for SEM implementation (Program Director) or an education reporter from the local newspaper. Separate participants into two groups and make sure that each group is out of earshot of other group. Distribute the interview simulation sheet applicable to each group (see Appendix C).

Visit the reporter group and explain that their mission in this simulation is to remain friendly and pleasant throughout the interview, but to put a negative spin in the headline for the article they would write. In other words, the administrator should leave the interview feeling great about the interview and confident that a positive headline will result when in fact a negative headline is the outcome. The reporter, while listening to the Program Director's responses, should think of a headline. For example, when hearing that the enrichment program is funded under the umbrella of special education, the resulting headline might be "Gifted Program Takes Funds From Special Education!"

Next visit with the Program Directors to make sure they understand it is their responsibility to tout how great their programs are.

Once participants understand their roles, they should separate into pairs (1 Program Director and 1 Reporter) and spend 15 minutes on the interview. If equipment is available, have each pair record the interview to review at a later time. After the interviews, everyone should comes back together for discussion. Ask for a pair to volunteer to be the first to share what occurred during the interview. First the Program Director should explain what he or she said to the Education Reporter. Then the Education Reporter should read the headline he or she has developed out loud. This process should continue until all of the pairs have presented.

Finally, participants should brainstorm strategies to minimize negative spin (build a relationship with the reporter, encourage students to take part in the interview, be prepared, know the reporter's bias, etc.).

Note: This activity can also be broken down into a two- or three-session activity:

Two-Session	Session One:	Simulation
	Session Two:	Discussion
Three-Session	Session One:	Simulation preparation: provide time for participants to think of possible questions and responses
	Session Two:	Simulation
	Session Three:	Discussion

Cultivating relationships with the media is important work and should not be overlooked. The following case study highlights the benefits of forming a relationship with a reporter from your local newspaper.

Reaching Out to the Media

When planning the orientation session for enrichment cluster facilitators, Ms. Berger, the building principal, and members of the Enrichment Team sent an invitation to the school reporter from the local newspaper. The team wanted the local community to know that the enrichment program maintains strong ties with the residents of the community and hoped the press coverage would generate wider support for the program. On the day of the orientation session, they were excited to host Rosemarie Moore, the school reporter. After greeting everyone and distributing nametags, Ms. Berger introduced Rosemarie and explained that she would be writing a brief overview of SEM and the enrichment cluster program for her column. When Ms. Berger began the session, she made sure not to use any educational jargon since Rosemarie and some of the facilitators were not teachers.

A parent member of the Enrichment Team stepped forward and, glancing at Rosemarie often, explained how the interest surveys that they administered to each student had helped shape the enrichment clusters offered for this cycle. After the introduction, the team divided participants into groups to take part in an enrichment cluster simulation. Ms. Berger and members of the Enrichment Team split themselves between the groups to facilitate discussion. Rosemarie moved from group to group, listening and writing, as participants explained how their interest in the enrichment cluster topic developed. Everyone became animated as they shared how their interest in the topic began as children and how they managed to sustain their interests into adulthood. Ms. Berger encouraged Rosemarie to tell everyone how she became interested in writing, and Rosemarie shared how she had always wanted to be a reporter. Rosemarie asked the Enrichment Team members many questions, particularly about the products or services they anticipated would result from cluster experiences and if they planned on showcasing the products in the future.

After each group of participants shared their simulated experiences and the team wrapped up the session with a discussion of management procedures, the orientation came to an end. As participants were leaving, Rosemarie approached Ms. Berger and announced, "I don't want to just write about this extraordinary program, I want to be a part of it!" Instead of simply writing about the orientation session and forgetting about it, Rosemarie became a facilitator for a popular journalism cluster. And Ms. Berger accomplished an important goal: She developed a relationship with a media contact to ensure that the community would continue to learn about the good work occurring in her school.

Strong schools translate into desirable communities. The strength of a school system is one of the most compelling reasons that people move to a specific area. As the leader of your school, seize every opportunity you can to promote your SEM program, activities, and accomplishments. If your school system celebrates successful programs at Board of Education meetings, suggest highlighting SEM. Figure 6.6 presents an announcement for a Board of Education presentation showcasing schoolwide enrichment.

BOARD OF EDUCATION MEETING
February 23, 2004

Dover Street School Auditorium

A SNAPSHOT OF ENRICHMENT
AT
THE DOVER STREET SCHOOL

PRESENTATIONS WILL BE MADE BY MEMBERS OF
THE DOVER STREET SCHOOL COMMUNITY

Principal Flanagan: Overview of the Schoolwide Enrichment Model

Kathy Tryor & Linda Scott: "A Growing Partnership"

<u>The Schoolwide Enrichment Model School Structures</u>

Cal Boone: The Regular Curriculum &

Differentiated Learning

Nancy Polen: Enrichment Clusters & High End Learning

Mark Blumberg: Continuum of Special Services

Closing Remarks

PTA President Travis: "Looking to the Future"

Figure 6.6. Announcement for a Board of Education presentation.

7

FUNDING

Once everyone shares the commitment for developing the talents and gifts of all students, then funding becomes a focus. Many professional development programs are slick expensive kits that can drain your budget allocation and leave little funding for other programs. You will find that SEM resources and materials do not cost a lot of money. Getting started packages containing books and videos cost around $100.00. Individual books and videos are available for much less, most within the $15.00 - $50.00 range. Support is also available on web sites (see Appendix D), including materials available for downloading and duplicating without a fee. Although SEM can be implemented on a shoestring budget, it is important to support SEM with adequate funding. Most SEM budgets include funds for an enrichment specialist at each site (either full or part time, depending on program needs), testing, resources, speakers, and other district-wide needs. If money is limited, you can start small. Following is a list of funding priorities:

- Full-time or part-time enrichment specialist
- Attendance at Confratute
- National Association for Gifted Children membership
- Resources and materials for professional development

Potential Sources of Funding

Some schools receive funds for SEM through the regular budgetary process. Schools may receive money that comes partially from state funds and partially from district funds based on the number of identified students participating in gifted programs. In addition, local mandates for changes in programs are usually accompanied by some funding.

When funding is limited, it is possible to successfully start programs by investing in key books and videotapes (see Appendix D) and sending one or two program leaders to Confratute. Sometimes principals within the same district can pool resources to purchase non-consumable materials to share between buildings. Central Offices can help here, too. Most districts have an administrative fund that can be tapped if central administrators know that the materials will be shared.

Even if your district does not have any funds available to support enrichment in your school, you need not feel that you cannot proceed. Many parents are happy to donate materials or canvas the neighborhood and area business for donations. Placing a list of needed materials in the teacher's faculty room is another way to solicit donations.

The No Child Left Behind (NCLB) Act may also be a source of funds. New allowable activities include use of NCLB funds for professional development, best practice models, gifted and talented education, and parent and community involvement—all areas that relate to SEM. The NCLB Act offers flexibility in the use of federal education funds because there is more attention on meeting students' needs by promoting innovative programs and less on red tape. Speak to your district central office administrators responsible for funding programs about tapping NCLB funds.

Whether you get monies from the district or state or not, you should still examine and pursue other sources of funding. For example, you can appeal to local Parent Teacher Associations. Tapping the local arts and humanities council to support different components of SEM is also sensible. If your school is near a university, consider reaching out to them. Don't be afraid to ask. Obtaining funds from sources other than the state or federal government often frees you from a lot of red tape, and you often have more say in how you use the money you receive.

Grants

Pursuing grants or corporate sponsorships to fund enrichment activities can be quite effective. Every successful grant written can become the basis for future proposals. (It is always a good idea to get central office approval before submitting a proposal to an outside funding source.)

The first step in preparing a successful grant is to develop a proposal: a formal request for SEM funds submitted to a specific funding source (e.g., government, corporation, or major foundation). A proposal must convey a clear purpose in a coherent well-organized manner. For example, you might write a grant requesting funding for parent awareness workshops, services for reaching at-risk students, professional development activities, curriculum development, program evaluation, field trips, mentoring programs, scholarships, summer enrichment programs, "loaned" executives to promote world-of-work awareness, public relations

"Our PTA will support SEM with money as long as they can see that it is having an effect on our students."

"We have yearly field trips to musical performances, ballet, art museums, health fairs, and career-related programs that are funded by community organizations."

campaigns promoting SEM, apprenticeship programs, equipment, and action research related to SEM implementation. Start by brainstorming a list of funding needs, and then select the most promising idea to develop in greater detail. (Don't forget to look at the strengths, interests, and backgrounds of those on your staff. It is not uncommon for teachers to have had a career before entering the teaching profession. One administrator told me that a first year teacher with corporate experience at IBM was interested in working with and mentoring teachers in technology. He was instrumental in applying for a technology grant.)

Once you have chosen a project, you need to write a proposal that clearly defines the process, the product, and the outcomes that you anticipate. The proposal should state that your request for funds is backed by research, what the current trends are in the field, and how these funds will fill an existing void in providing enrichment opportunities to more students. Be sure to include how you will evaluate the success of the program or initiative proposed.

Make your proposal stand out by expressing the educational philosophy and vision of your school community. Call upon your Schoolwide Enrichment Planning Team for assistance. The more stakeholders that you involve and reference in the proposal, the greater the chance that your proposal will be seriously considered. Following is an example of how a little research can help you write successful grants, and Appendix B includes a successful grant requesting funds for implementing SEM in a southeastern school in Connecticut.

"We wrote a grant that provides $77,777 per year for three years. It provides funding for total staff development, instructional supplies, consultants, and some equipment. It will carry us through the implementation process. I am now beginning to look at alternative funding for our middle school."

Tapping Alternative Funding

Ms. Brodem, the principal of the Ketchum School, was excited that her colleagues were on board and ready to begin implementing SEM. As she was driving to school, she thought about how to carry them through the implementation process. She knew there was not enough funding available through the traditional sources. The district budget was strictly bare bones. The local taxes has been steadily on the rise the last two years, and the chief financial officer for the district let all administrators know that this was not the year to begin any new programs or to purchase any new materials.

Undeterred, Ms. Brodem considered reaching out to the community to fund aspects of SEM. She knew that the CEO of the town's largest corporation was a real music buff. In the past, she had always made sure that he was invited to the annual school music concert and play. He was always delighted to attend and had told her that if there was anything he could do for her or the students, she should contact him.

Before approaching the CEO, Ms. Brodem checked the corporation's web site and learned that the CEO's love for the arts was reflected in the corporation's giving history (the programs that the corporation regularly contributed to). Ms. Brodem felt that if she submitted a proposal requesting support for expanding the school's limited arts program, her proposal would be received enthusiastically. She made sure to include items she new the CEO valued and requested funds for a comprehensive artist-in-residence program, new stage and lighting equipment, and body microphones.

Working with the presidents of the PTA and SEPTA (the special education parent-teacher association) and the newly formed Schoolwide Enrichment Team, Ms. Brodem developed a proposal that stressed that all students would have the opportunity to participate in the expanded program. The proposal detailed how SEM encourages creative productivity by exposing students to various areas of interests and fields of study not typically found in the school's curriculum. It included a comprehensive explanation of Type I, Type II, and Type III activities and provided examples of how a student who becomes interested in performing in a play after a Type I experience might pursue additional training and choose to put on a one-man show to present what he has learned. The proposal also emphasized how students will develop a sense of creative accomplishment and self-confidence. Finally, the proposal showed the connection between state learning standards and specific activities in which students would be engaged.

Within weeks, Ms. Brodem received word that the proposal was accepted. At a series of celebratory faculty and PTA meetings, she announced that the school would receive $10,000 a year for five years to develop SEM in the school.

Convincing those who control the purse strings and make decisions about funds is an important aspect of your work. Be relentless in getting out the message that opportunities for your students to participate in escalating levels of enrichment is fundamental to helping them develop their individual potentials in creative and productive ways.

8

THE SEM ADMINISTRATOR

Being an administrator is not easy. With mandates continuously changing, pressure from the school community to raise test scores, and the uncertainties about how best to prepare students for a world we can only imagine, it's no wonder that administrators often feel like piñatas. However, remaining steadfast in your resolve to provide enrichment opportunities, resources, and services to develop student strengths and interests will reap great rewards. And there are other characteristics you can develop to help you implement SEM successfully.

Don't Be a Loner

Being a good leader is a not about being the lone person at the helm, steering toward a land you alone have deemed a good destination for everyone on board your ship. Instead, being a leader is more about shepherding, bringing a group of people together who all have a common aim and helping the group achieve that aim. As you begin to consider SEM for your school, form a steering committee comprised of the stakeholders who would be affected by the decision to implement (e.g., teachers, parents, students) and work with them to decide whether or not the school is ready to embrace the concepts of SEM. If you show them that you are committed to building consensus and are willing to take a team approach to work through any issues and challenges that may arise, then you have laid the groundwork for successful implementation. Figure 8.1 presents a memorandum written by a principal to a central office detailing the recommendation for an SEM adoption.

If your school has a mandate for SEM, then you should still consider forming a steering committee as a way to build trusting relationships. If possible, invite

Administrator's Library
—
The Steering Committee

See pp. 40-43 in The Schoolwide Enrichment Model: A How-to Guide for Educational Excellence

---

Southbay Elementary School

To: Dr. Benning, Director of Curriculum and Instruction
From: Mr. Frankel, Principal and Chair of the Gifted and Talented Committee
Re: Steering Committee Recommendation: The Schoolwide Enrichment Model

The mission of the district steering committee has been accomplished. Our discussions on how we can better address the unique needs of our high-ability youngsters and our research into various enrichment programs has led us to the conclusion that the Schoolwide Enrichment Model is our model of choice. In order to learn more about the best way to implement the model, the committee is requesting funding for a team of administrators, teachers, and parents to attend Confratute, the summer institute on enrichment programming held at the University of Connecticut in July. A brochure explaining Confratute is attached. At Confratute, the committee will continue to meet and fine-tune a presentation that, as agreed, will be presented at the September Board of Education meeting. The full committee report will be in your hands by the end of the week.
Thank you!

Figure 8.1. Memorandum to central office recommending SEM.

staff members who have a positive outlook, lots of energy, and a can-do attitude. This committee can help you introduce the model to your wider school community, making the mandate to implement SEM less like a directive from a "voice from above" and more like a team effort.

Know SEM

As you embark on the implementation journey, make sure you have a thorough knowledge of SEM and understand the relationship between SEM and general education. General educators have become much more receptive to the tenets of enrichment learning and teaching as the pressure to raise standards for all students has increased, and you need to be able to speak to them about infusing high-end learning experiences into their classrooms in ways that make sense to them. Know how the SEM Structures (Regular Curriculum, Enrichment Clusters, and Continuum of Services) fit your school program and educate your stakeholders about the Service Delivery Components (Total Talent Portfolio, curriculum modification techniques, and enrichment learning and teaching practices). You can set the standard for your staff by participating in professional development activities.

Be Organized

Working within your Schoolwide Enrichment Professional Development Plan will help you achieve your goals. Although you will be working with the Schoolwide Enrichment Planning Team, the ultimate responsibility rests with you. Be detail oriented and keep everyone on track.

Raise Expectations

While providing remediation for students who struggle academically is something you must do, understand that if you guide your staff to become predominantly "fixers" instead of "enrichers," you will be doing all of your students a great disservice. Raise the level of expectation for all students. View your school through the lens of enrichment and support your teachers as they move toward tapping all students' interests and strengths. Guided by state learning standards and district mission statements, show that you are committed to a rigorous, meaningful, intellectually challenging program for all students.

Be Flexible

While SEM in its entirety may be appealing to you, you may need to make some modifications to the program until you gain greater trust and commitment from your stakeholders. Some administrators like to begin with enrichment clusters because it often ignites the flame of enthusiasm. If you decide to follow this path, test the political waters and make certain that you have enough willing participants. If any staff members have concerns about their roles, schedule a time to meet with them. Explain that you are willing to make adjustments in response to their concerns. Using a flexible approach that is true to the philosophy and the goals of the model supports implementation.

Be Creative

If the teachers in your school are like most, you will surely hear from some skeptics about the program: "How will we be able to cover the regular curriculum?" "What will happen to my specials?" "How can I keep adding new programs to my already overburdened teaching load?" While there are no easy answers, listening to their concerns and adjusting the workload and scheduling patterns to provide ways for everyone to participate in SEM is your goal. One principal arranged a grade level meeting after hearing teachers complain that there just wasn't enough time to do everything they had planned to do. She wore surgical gloves to the meeting to show a sense of humor as well as her commitment to help them remove redundancies in the curriculum to make time for the more impressive enrichment learning experiences they wanted to plan. See Figure 8.2 for an advertisement promoting a recess enrichment opportunity for students. This creative approach to bringing Type I experiences into a jam packed schedule is a terrific

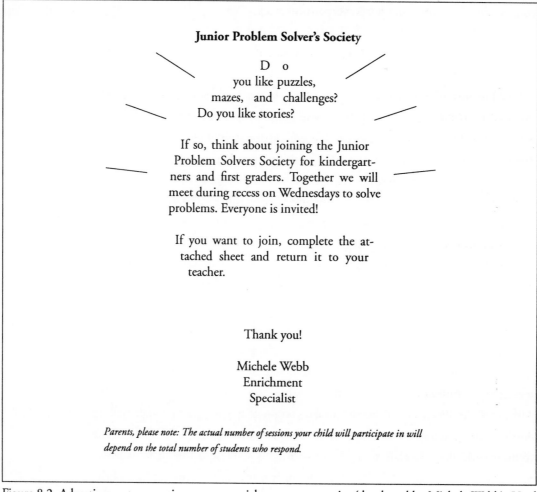

Junior Problem Solver's Society

D o
you like puzzles,
mazes, and challenges?
Do you like stories?

If so, think about joining the Junior Problem Solvers Society for kindergartners and first graders. Together we will meet during recess on Wednesdays to solve problems. Everyone is invited!

If you want to join, complete the attached sheet and return it to your teacher.

Thank you!

Michele Webb
Enrichment
Specialist

Parents, please note: The actual number of sessions your child will participate in will depend on the total number of students who respond.

Figure 8.2. Advertisement promoting a recess enrichment opportunity (developed by Michele Webb). Used with permission.

example of creative thinking.

Have a Sense of Humor

Part of your role is to act as cheerleader. A program can be made or broken simply by the way you act. Laughter eases tensions and encourages cooperation. Barry Roberts, humorist and author of Practice Safe Stress (2000) states that a sense of humor can help people become more creative, productive, and efficient if they use it to minimize day-to-day stresses. If you do everything that you can to approach the work with enthusiasm and a sense of humor, your attitude will spread. Don't allow the stress of making changes to have a negative effect on your attitude and on what you hope to accomplish. (For more information on Barry Roberts book and his seminars, visit www.practicesafestress.com.)

Be Confident

It is in your best interest to avoid being overly influenced by local politics and issues of accountability. If you believe in the concepts of SEM, don't buckle under pressure from naysayers. Appearing insecure is not conducive to success. Instead, anticipate problems and develop strategies to overcome roadblocks. Be vocal about how SEM matches other initiatives and promotes the standards in your school. Be proactive about getting the word out.

Be a Collaborator

Successful administrators are good communicators who collaborate with their staff and encourage staff to expand their beliefs and ideas. Foster an environment in your school that supports open, ongoing professional conversations about the ever-changing needs of your students and be mindful of the difficulties the shift to SEM will bring for some. If teachers know that they can count on your support, they will be more inclined to forge ahead. Maintain a risk-free environment by assuring them that you won't formally evaluate their enrichment strategies and lesson plans. Encourage them to try an enrichment strategy during a formal classroom observation, but don't include your feedback in the write-up. Instead, discuss what you have observed and make suggestions in a collegial conversation. Be sure to compliment the teacher for being professional and forward thinking.

Follow Through

Sometimes you have to "bite the bullet" with teachers whose enrichment and instructional experiences remain marginal at best. If collaboration and support do not get teachers to improve their teaching strategies, it is time for you to incorporate your expectations into a formal evaluation. Remember that students come first, and it is your responsibility to make sure that all the students in your school are getting the best possible education.

Be Public Relations Savvy

Knowing how to sustain good public relations with staff, the media, and parents are strengths, and having the ability to persevere through controversy is a must. Throughout the implementation process, smart administrators will play up as often as possible what SEM can do for students, the staff, and the community at large.

Communicate with Other SEM Administrators

Staying in touch with other administrators is nothing short of essential. You can and should bounce ideas off of or share experiences with other administrators implementing SEM by attending conferences and workshops that offer presentations about gifted education, enrichment learning, and teaching practices. Even if you find it difficult to attend workshops or conferences, with the Internet at your fingertips, there is no reason to work in isolation. Some administrators have created web sites or joined list serves to present and discuss ideas. The following web sites provide up-to-date information about SEM:

- The Neag Center for Gifted Education and Talent Development (www.gifted.uconn.edu)
- The National Association for Gifted Children (www.nagc.org)
- The National Research Center on the Gifted and Talented (www.gifted.uconn.edu/nrcgt.html)

9

PULLING IT ALL TOGETHER

The implementation process is like a living thing; it requires much care and attention and no two schools will have the same experiences. This chapter is intended to serve as a quick guide to the steps to successful implementation. There are five major areas on which you need to focus: developing a plan, establishing teacher buy-in, communicating with parents and community, securing funding, and monitoring progress. Figure 9.1 outlines these areas. Though I provide a number of tips and suggestions in this chapter, keep in mind that being flexible and responding to the needs of your staff and students will help you nurture SEM's growth in your school.

Develop a Plan

Organize a Schoolwide Enrichment Planning Team

If you do not already have a site-based management team that could serve as the Schoolwide Enrichment Planning Team, invite teachers, parents, and students (if appropriate) to join you as you work to implement SEM. You may even want to invite a critic of SEM to show that you are willing to address concerns and work with everyone.

Once you have gathered a team, your first job will be to arrange an awareness session for the team members. Introduce the team members to the model, the research behind it, and how SEM has the capacity to raise standards and, ultimately, your students' achievement.

Show How SEM Fits with Other Initiatives

Compare the language associated with SEM to language in district/state doc-

---

Steps for Successful Implementation

I. Develop a Plan
- Organize a Schoolwide Enrichment Planning Team
- Show how SEM fits with other initiatives
- Develop a planning document

II. Establish Teacher Buy-in
- Build relationships
- Conduct an awareness session for teachers
- Avoid administrivia
- Be sensitive to constraints on time
- Be open to concerns and suggestions
- Send teachers to Confratute
- Celebrate success

III. Communicate with Parents and Community
- Introduce SEM to parents and the community
- Communicate realistic goals
- Say thank you
- Arrange for students to make PTA/PTO presentations
- Maintain media contact

IV. Secure Funding
- Make the case for funding

V. Monitor Progress
- Stick to a viable timeline
- Be a coach
- Take a look at your school
- Shadow a student

Figure 9.1. Outline for successful implementation.

uments detailing school improvement initiatives. Point out that the purpose of state learning standards is to prepare children to function at their highest levels once they leave school. Make the point that SEM brings the standards alive in the school setting.

Develop a Planning Document

As a team, develop planning documents for your school's professional development activities. This document may detail month-by-month or year-by-year implementation plans.

Establish Teacher Buy-in

Build Relationships

Being a principal is a relationship, not a role, and building a relationship with your staff will contribute to the establishment of a culture in your school that fosters kinship and togetherness. When you take the time to talk with your colleagues, you will find a host of similarities among faculty members' reasons for becoming educators and beliefs about what is good for the students in your school. If you come away from these conversations knowing more about the experiences you staff had in school as young learners and who may have influenced them to enter the teaching profession, then you are setting the stage for improved teacher buy-in. Providing them with opportunities to think back to the gifts they may have received from a former teacher or other significant person in their lives can lead them to think about the gifts they can bring their students. Every meeting between a young person and an educator can be a unique exchange of gifts with everlasting positive effects for all involved. You can show them how SEM can be the vehicle for sharing and developing gifts.

Conduct an Awareness Session for Teachers

Have the teacher members of the Schoolwide Enrichment Planning Team arrange an awareness session for their peers. If you have an enrichment specialist, ask him or her to serve as a consultant teacher to follow up on issues that come up in the awareness session.

Avoid Administrivia

You may feel compelled to use faculty meeting time to cover an array of "administrivia" items, attending to day-to-day details that ensure that your school runs smoothly. However, faculty meeting time is precious time. It isn't often that you have the opportunity to spend time together as a group. One way to communicate with staff more efficiently and to buy time in faculty meetings for professional conversations is to use a system of routing slips. Not only will you free up valuable faculty meeting time, you will drastically reduce the amount of paper that you distribute to your staff. Three times during the school day (during morning arrival, lunchtime, and the end of the day), post routing slips communicating important information in a designated area for teachers to peruse. The routing slip is usually one copy of a memorandum that details your message with a staff roster attached. Teachers respond by initialing or, if appropriate, by writing a response to your prompt. For example, you may inform the staff that you are showing the video *A Rising Tide Lifts All Ships* (Renzulli, 1997) on a particular morning and that refreshments will be served. Teachers can indicate whether they will attend by writing yes or no next to their name. Or perhaps you need to explain a directive from Central Office. You can post it as a routing slip and have staff members initial that they read the notice. This procedure also enables the office staff to follow up with anyone who may have missed the notice. One piece of paper in lieu of memorandums placed in each mailbox is a much more efficient way of communicating and opens up tremendously exciting possibilities for faculty meeting

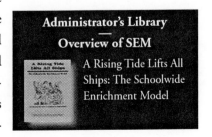

Administrator's Library
Overview of SEM

A Rising Tide Lifts All Ships: The Schoolwide Enrichment Model

---

Springs Elementary School

To: All Teachers
From: Ms. Bailey, Principal
Re: Spotlighting Our Student's Talents

Next month's faculty meeting will be a celebration of sorts. Since SEM has become so much a part of the philosophy of our school and we are all so excited about the changes we have seen in student motivation, I am arranging this opportunity for you to share your successes and samples of student work that illustrate their talents, strengths, and interests. This informal faculty meeting will take place in the Library-Media Center. Each discussion group will include a teacher from each grade level so that you all can hear about the wonderful things happening in our building across grade levels. Special area teachers and support staff will join the groups. Bring your appetite. Breakfast treats will be served!

Name	Signature	Comments
Steve Burns	*Steve Burns*	*I'll be slightly delayed.*
Joan Pennington	*Joan Pennington*	*Looking forward to this!*

Johnsonville High School
English Department

Some of us will be meeting in the Library Media Center on Thursday at 8:00 a.m. to discuss how to develop gifted behaviors in more of our students. If you are not quite sure how to go about encouraging talent development, this meeting will be a great opportunity to share your thoughts and get ideas from other colleagues. Please sign below if you wish to join us. Coffee, tea and assorted breakfast treats will be provided!

Name	Signature	Comments
Andrea Axelrod	*Andrea Axelrod*	*I'll be there.*
Sue Benton	*Sue Benton*	*Sorry, can't make it.*

Figure 9.2. Two sample routing slips.

agendas. See Figure 9.2 for two samples of routing slips.

Be Sensitive to Time Constraints

One of the main criticisms that you may hear from your teachers is that "they don't have time to do something else." A closer look at your existing curriculum may give you insight into why your teachers' feel they are overloaded. As part of the implementation process, you may want to take as long as one full year to determine exactly what is taught across grade levels and ferret out gaps in instruction or topics that are taught time and time again (Hayes Jacobs, 1997, 2004). You can fine tune the curriculum so that it flows more efficiently and then begin to infuse Type I, Type II and Type III experiences into your existing curriculum.

Be Open to Concerns and Suggestions

It is your responsibility to help teachers ease into this new way of looking at their students. Be a good listener and respond to their concerns. Using surveys, discussions, and observations, find out how they are experiencing the program. Develop a systematic method for evaluating how the program is growing from the teachers' perspectives and use the information to help new teachers adapt to the program. In *The Schoolwide Enrichment Model* (Renzulli & Reis, 1997) there are multiple references to evaluation that will assist you in providing a defensible program.

Administrator's Library
Evaluation
See the Conclusion in The Schoolwide Enrichment Model: A How-to Guide for Educational Excellence

Send Teachers to Confratute

Consider sending some of your teachers to Confratute for further professional development. Administrators often talk about the benefits of a "grass roots spread," and teachers who attend Confratute typically return to their school systems so charged up and ready for full implementation that it will take real discipline not to move too quickly. Their colleagues will soon be asking to attend as the word about SEM begins to spread.

Celebrate Success

Make time to celebrate implementation successes at faculty meetings, student assemblies, and district-wide professional development sessions. Help teachers take note of their students' engagement in activities and their overall improved enthusiasm about school. Compliment your colleagues on their commitment to their students and recognize them for taking the initiative to look critically at their instructional practices with an eye toward making positive changes.

Communicate with Parents and Community

Introduce SEM to Parents and the Community

Just as you encouraged teacher members of your planning team to present to their colleagues, do the same with parents. Use any parent forum possible; PTA and PTO meetings are usually great opportunities to introduce parents to SEM. Once parents become aware of the benefits of the model and the positive effects SEM can have on their children's ability to learn well, there won't be anything stopping them!

Encourage parents to get involved in the program. Invite them to share their interests and talents with the children. Figure 9.3 presents a sample flyer requesting volunteers.

Bellows Elementary School
Top Ten Interests 2003-2004
Totals for Grades 2 - 5

1. Magic
2. Animals
3. Sports, Learning New Games
4. Volcanoes & Earthquakes
5. Math Games & Puzzlers
6. Dinosaurs & Fossils
7. Drawing
8. Arts & Crafts
9. Life in the Ocean
10. Computers & Technology

We Invite You to Share Your Interests!

Do you share any of the interests listed above? Do you have an expertise in another topic you think our students might be interested in learning about? If so, please return the slip below by January 12th or contact Marcia Berger, Chairperson of the Schoolwide Enrichment Team at the Bellows School.

- - - - - - - - - - Tear off and return to your child's teacher. - - - - - - - - - -

☐ Yes, I may be interested in sharing my experience(s) with students. Please contact me with more information about how I may be able to participate.

My name:_____Child's name_____
Best number at which to reach me is:_____
My area(s) of interests and/or expertise are:_____
_____.

Figure 9.3. Flyer requesting volunteers.

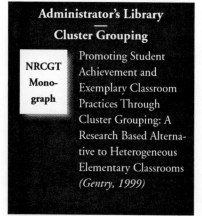

Administrator's Library
Cluster Grouping

NRCGT Monograph

Promoting Student Achievement and Exemplary Classroom Practices Through Cluster Grouping: A Research Based Alternative to Heterogeneous Elementary Classrooms *(Gentry, 1999)*

Communicate Realistic Goals

Sometimes parents get so excited and enthusiastic that they don't want to endure long term planning goals. They don't want to wait three years for their child to receive the full benefits of SEM. Therefore, be sure to demonstrate to parents how their child will benefit almost immediately from each phase of implementation. Consider a cluster group option to reduce issues associated with long term planning if you cannot provide the necessary professional development for all of your teachers at the same time. Or, consider beginning with the enrichment cluster component of the model where all of the children reap the benefits of high-end learning experiences.

Say Thank You!

Remember to acknowledge community members who volunteer their time for the programs in your school. Figure 9.4 presents a thank you letter written to an Academy of Inquiry and Talent Development facilitator (who happened to be the Mayor).

NORTHERN MIDDLE SCHOOL

March 23, 2004

Dear Mayor Shine:

Thank you for facilitating the Leadership Academy this year at Northern Middle School. It was very generous of you to share your time, expertise, and enthusiasm with our students. We are very proud of our Academies of Inquiry and Talent Development Program and we are always working to improve and further develop our programming to serve our students better. The success of this program relies on the facilitators who give so unselfishly of themselves. Thank you for all of your contributions.

Please reserve 3:30-4:30 p.m. on May 4th to help us celebrate the culmination of this year's program. At the Academy Celebration, we will have the opportunity to acknowledge your contributions. In April, you will receive a formal invitation with specific details.

We look forward to the opportunity to more formally thank you and the other facilitators on May 4th. See you then!

Sincerely,

Justin Feingold, Principal   Anthony Dawkins, Enrichment Specialist

---

Figure 9.4. Sample thank you letter.

Arrange for Students to Make PTA/PTO Presentations on Aspects of SEM

Parents always love to see their children participate in presentations and you should do everything you can to involve students in parent meetings. See Figure 9.5 for a letter written to the PTA requesting the opportunity to showcase the products students developed after participating in a Type I experience arranged by the PTA Cultural Arts Committee.

Maintain Media Contact

Building relationships and maintaining contact with the media is critical to your success. Reporters and their audiences are always more attentive if they can see themselves in the story. The more you know about your local media people, the better your chance of getting positive media coverage.

Contemplate Funding Sources

Make the Case for Funding

SEM can be implemented on less money than many other programs, but funding is always an issue. Once you can show how the language of the model matches the language in your state and district standards, you can more easily make the case for funding. Getting SEM included in your annual budget and tapping state, district and teacher center grants, PTA/PTO sources, and corporate sponsorships are all viable ways to fund SEM. Your funding priorities should in-

---

Greenbelt Elementary School

November 12, 2003

Dear Mrs. Garrett, PTA President, and Members of the Executive Board:

Every parent knows that an interested child is a good learner, and the staff of Greenbelt Elementary School is committed to keeping our youngsters excited about learning. Toward that end, I am requesting the opportunity to present some of the wonderful products that our students have produced after being exposed to some of the Type I exploratory experiences that you arranged through the Cultural Arts Committee. A small group of children and members of our Enrichment Team will be available on the evening of the next PTA meeting, and I promise you will be amazed at the quality of what you will see. Many thanks for your continued support.

Sincerely,

Mr. Walker
Principal
Greenbelt Elementary School
jpo

Figure 9.5. Letter requesting the opportunity to present SEM products at a PTA meeting.

clude an enrichment specialist, Confratute attendance, NAGC membership, and resources and materials for professional development.

Monitor Progress

Amidst all the activity and details of getting a program going, it is important take a step back and look at the bigger picture. Ask yourself, "Am I meeting my deadline for implementation? Are my colleagues handling the changes well? Are parents receptive and involved? Are students excited to come to school?"

Use Your Timeline

Use your timeline to monitor progress. Are tasks being successfully completed on time? If not, reassess your implementation strategies and whether all your stakeholders are ready to move forward through the implementation stages. You may not be providing enough time to make changes. Don't be afraid to revise the timeline in response to needs you see. Giving the gift of time will foster the trust you need to promote effective learning.

Be a Coach

Remember that most teachers do not have a background in gifted education and very few ever learned during pre-service education how to meet the unique learning needs of high-ability learners. It is your job to support them by providing them with pertinent articles about SEM, opportunities for coaching and professional development, and by conducting formal and informal conversations about aspects of the model as it relates to their specific classrooms and students. As the next case study shows, finding time to allow teachers to "grow" SEM at their own pace can lead to great success.

The Gift of Time

Dr. Daniels, principal of Jeffersonville Elementary, saw her role in her school as that of a coach and a facilitator. She believed that teachers are the driving forces behind good school programs, and the best way to encourage her staff to achieve their best was to give them time as a group to reflect on their work and how it impacted their students. Dr. Daniels provided teachers with many opportunities to share triumphs and frustrations. She encouraged teachers to establish their own support groups without administrative presence during which they could share student work and receive feedback from colleagues with whom they felt comfortable. In addition, Dr. Daniels organized regularly scheduled debriefing sessions during which teachers shared with each other and with members of the administration both positive reactions to the SEM program as well as any frustrations and lack of understanding they had about SEM. Acting as a coach to her staff instead of a dictator, Dr. Daniels was able to support her staff through some difficult periods and together, they were able to make Jeffersonville Elementary a true SEM school within a few years.

Take a Look at Your School

One day, after students and staff have all gone home, take a walk around your building to see if you get a sense that the principles of enrichment learning and teaching are discernible. Would your emphasis on student-centered, engaged learning be apparent to a visitor? Does the student work on display indicate that your students are producing at levels commensurate with their abilities and that all of your students are given opportunities to do so? If your answers are "yes" then you are well on your way to becoming a successful SEM school!

Shadow a Student

Your students' accomplishments are products of the opportunities and expectation that you and your colleagues hold for them. Follow around one of your more able students for a few hours. Is the instructional program a good match for his or her ability? Show interest by talking to your students about their projects and take note of their feelings about their work. Shadowing a student can be a wonderful form of data collection!

This Is Only the Beginning

As you contemplate the wide range of attitudes and unique qualities inherent in your existing school structures, remain committed to adapting the model to fit your school and community. You don't need to implement SEM in a "cookie cutter" manner, and an SEM program will develop differently in every school. As long as you remain steadfast in your commitment to the philosophy and the goals of SEM, you will succeed. And as the public debate continues, the proof of success will be found where it has always rested, in the lives and the accomplishments of the children.

REFERENCES

American Association of University Women Educational Foundation. (1992). *How schools short-change girls.* Washington, DC: Author.

Beck, J. (1992). Mainstream drowns gifted students. *The NCGAT Newsletter, 16*(2), 3-5.

Brown, C. N. (1997). Gifted identification as a constitutional issue. *Roeper Review, 19,* 157-160.

Creative Learning Press. (1997). *A rising tide lifts all ships: The schoolwide enrichment model* [Video]. Available from Creative Learning Press, PO Box 320, Mansfield Center, CT 06250.

Delisle, J. (2003, November). *Highly gifted, barely served: The legacy of inclusion.* Strand session presented at the annual meeting of the National Association for Gifted Children Conference: Indianapolis, Indiana.

Dodd, D. (1987). Point-counterpoint: Special without special education. *Journal for the Education of the Gifted, 10,* 65-77.

Friedman, N. G. (2003). Talent development with English language learners. In W.A. Owings & L.S. Kaplan (Eds.), *Best practices, best thinking, and emerging issues in school leadership.* (pp.147-153). Thousand Oaks, CA: Corwin Press.

Ford, D. (1999). Renzulli's philosophy and program: Opening doors and nurturing potential. *Journal for the Education of the Gifted, 23*(1), 117-124.

Ford D., & Frazier, M. (1999, November). *Into the millennium: New directions for gifted education.* Panel discussion presented at the annual meeting of the National Association for Gifted Children Conference, Albuquerque, NM.

Gardner, H. (1983). *Frames of mind.* NY: Basic Books.

Gardner, H. (1993). *Multiple intelligences: The theory in practice, a reader.* NY: BasicBooks.

Gentry, M. L. (1999). *Promoting student achievement and exemplary classroom practices through cluster grouping: A research-based alternative to heterogeneous elementary classrooms.* Storrs, Connecticut: The National Research Center on the Gifted and Talented.

Gifted and Talented Students Education Act of 1999. H.R. 637 & S.505, 106th Cong. (1999).

Hale-Benson, J. (1986). *Black children: Their roots, culture and learning styles.* Baltimore: The John Hopkins University Press.

Hayes Jacobs, H. (1997). *Mapping the big picture: Integrating curriculum and assessment K-12.* Alexandria, VA: Association for Curriculum and Development.

Hayes Jacobs, H. (Ed.). (2004). *Getting results with curriculum mapping.* Alexandria, VA: Association for Curriculum and Development.

Irvine, D. J. (1991). Gifted education without a state mandate: The importance of vigorous advocacy. *Gifted Child Quarterly, 35*(4), 196-199.

Jacob K. Javits Gifted and Talented Students Education Act of 1988, 20 U.S.C. §3061 et seq.

Jellen, H. G. (1985). Renzulli's enrichment scheme for the gifted: Educational accommodation of the gifted in the American context. *Gifted Education International, 3*(1), 12-17.

Johnsen, S. K. (1999). Renzulli's model: Needed research. *Journal for the Education of the Gifted, 23*(1), 102-116.

Kontos, S., Carter, K. R., Ormrod, J. E., & Cooney, J. B. (1983). Reversing the revolving door: A strict interpretation of Renzulli's definition of giftedness. *Roeper Review, 35,* 35-38.

Marland, S. (1972). *Education of the gifted and talented.* Report to Congress. Washington, DC: U.S.Government Printing Office.

National Association for Gifted Children (1998). *Pre-k—Grade 12 gifted program standards.* Washington, DC: Author.

No Child Left Behind Act of 2001, 20 U.S.C. §6301 et seq.

O'Connell, P. (2003). "Federal involvement in gifted and talented education." In N. Colangelo and G. A. Davis (Eds.). *Handbook of gifted education (3rd ed.)* (pp. 604-608). Boston: Allyn & Bacon.

Olszewski-Kubilius, P. (1999). A critique of Renzulli's theory into practice models for gifted learners. *Journal for the Education of the Gifted, 23*(1), 55-66.

Pendarvis, E., Howley, C., & Howley, A. (1999). Renzulli's triad: school to work for gifted students. *Journal for the Education of the Gifted, 23*(1), 75-86.

Purcell, J. H. (1993, Fall). A study of the status of programs for high ability students. *The National Research Center on the Gifted and Talented Newsletter,* 6-7.

Reis, S. M., Burns, D. E., & Renzulli, J. R. (1992). *Curriculum compacting: The complete guide to modifying the regular curriculum for high ability students.* Mansfield Center, CT: Creative Learning Press, Inc.

Renzulli, J. S. (1977). *The enrichment triad model: A guide for developing defensible programs for the gifted and talented.* Mansfield Center, CT: Creative Learning Press.

Renzulli, J. S. (1978). *What makes giftedness? Reexamining a definition.* Chronicle Guidance Professional Service, P991, 1-4, NY: Chronicle Guidance Publications, Inc.

Renzulli, J. S. (1997). *Interest-A-Lyzer.* Mansfield Center, CT: Creative Learning Press.

Renzulli, J. S. (2002). A practical plan for identifying gifted and talented students. In J. S. Renzulli, L. H. Smith, A. J. White, C. M. Callahan, R. K. Hartman & K. L. Westberg, *Scales for rating the behavioral characteristics of superior students (revised edition)* pp. 46-54. Mansfield Center, CT: Creative Learning Press.

Renzulli, J. S., Gentry, M. & Reis, S. M. (2003). *Enrichment clusters: A practical plan for real world student-driven learning.* Mansfield Center, CT: Creative Learning Press.

Renzulli, J. S., & Reis, S. M. (1985). *The schoolwide enrichment model: A comprehensive plan for educational excellence.* Mansfield Center, CT: Creative Learning Press.

Renzulli, J. S., & Reis, S. M. (1994). Research related to the schoolwide enrichment triad model. *Gifted Child Quarterly, 38*(1), 7-19.

Renzulli, J. S., & Reis, S. M. (1997). *The schoolwide enrichment model: A how-to guide for educational excellence (2nd ed.).* Mansfield Center, CT: Creative Learning Press.

Renzulli, J. S., & Reis, S. M. (2001, April). The schoolwide enrichment model: A school improvement plan that achieves excellence without elitism [Brochure]. Mansfield Center, CT: Creative Workshop Associates.

Renzulli, J. S., Reis, S. M., & Smith, L. H. (1981). *The revolving door identification model.*

Mansfield Center, CT: Creative Learning Press.

Renzulli, J. S., Smith, L. H., White, A. J., Callahan, C. M., & Hartman, R. K. (1976). *Scales for rating the behavioral characteristics of superior students.* Mansfield Center, CT: Creative Learning Press.

Renzulli, J. S., Smith, L. H., White, A. J., Callahan, C. M., Hartman, R. K., & Westberg, K. L. (2002). *Scales for rating the behavioral characteristics of superior students (revised edition).* Mansfield Center, CT: Creative Learning Press.

Renzulli, J. S., Smith, L. H., White, A. J., Callahan, C. M., Hartman, R. K., Westberg, K. L., Gavin, M. K., Reis, S. M., Siegle, D., & Sytsma, R. E. (2004). *Scales for rating the behavioral characteristics of superior students (revised edition).* Mansfield Center, CT: Creative Learning Press.

Resnick, L. B. (1987). *Education and learning to think.* Washington, DC: National Academies Press.

Roberts, B. (2000). *Practice safe stress: A guide to using your inner sense of humor to minimize day-to-day stress.* NY: Barry Roberts, Inc.

Ross, P. O., United States Department of Education, Office of Educational Research and Improvement. (1993). *National excellence: A case for developing america's talent.* Report No.: PIP-93-1201. Washington, DC: U.S. Government Printing Office.

Shade, B. J. (1994). Understanding the African-American learner. In E.R. Hollins, J.E. King, W.C. Hayman (Eds.), *Teaching diverse populations: Formulating a knowledge base.* (pp.175-189). New York: State University of New York.

Starko, A. J. (1986). *Its about time.* Mansfield Center, CT: Creative Learning Press.

Sternberg, R. J. (1985). A componential theory of intellectual giftedness. *Gifted Child Quarterly, 25,* 86-93.

Sternberg, R. J. (1999). Rising tides and racing torpedoes: Triumphs and tribulations of the adult gifted as illustrated by the career of Joseph Renzulli. *Journal for the Education of the Gifted, 23*(1), 67.

Sternberg, R. J. & Davidson, J. E. (1986). *Conceptions of giftedness.* NY: Cambridge University Press.

Terman, L. (1925). *Mental and physical traits of a thousand gifted children.* Stanford, CA: Stanford University Press.

Terman, L. (1959). *The gifted group at mid-life.* Stanford, CA: Stanford University Press.

Tirozzi, G. (2003). Politics and education: A conundrum for school leadership. In W.A. Owings & L. S. Kaplan (Eds.), *Best practices, best thinking, and emerging issues in school leadership.* (p 53). Thousand Oaks, CA: Corwin Press.

Torrance, E. P., & Sisk, D. A. (1997). *Gifted and talented children in the regular classroom.* Buffalo, NY: Creative Education Foundation Press.

Whitmore, J. (1987). Conceptualizing the issue of underserved populations of gifted students. *Journal for the Education of the Gifted, 10,* 141-153.

APPENDIX A: EXECUTIVE SUMMARY

The Schoolwide Enrichment Model[1]
Executive Summary[2]

Joseph S. Renzulli and Sally M. Reis
University of Connecticut, Storrs, Connecticut, USA

Introduction

Enrichment programs for gifted and talented students have been the true laboratories of the world's schools because they have presented ideal opportunities for testing new ideas and experimenting with potential solutions to long-standing educational problems. Programs for high potential students have been an especially fertile place for experimentation because such programs are not usually encumbered by prescribed curriculum guides or traditional methods of instruction. It was within the context of these programs that the thinking skills movement first took hold in American education, and the pioneering work of notable theorists such as Benjamin Bloom, Howard Gardner, and Robert Sternberg first gained the attention of the education community. Other developments that had their origins in special programs are currently being examined for general practice. These developments include: a focus on concept rather than skill learning, the use of interdisciplinary curriculum and theme-based studies, student portfolios, performance assessment, cross-grade grouping, alternative scheduling patterns, and perhaps most important, opportunities for students to exchange traditional roles as lesson-learners and doers-of-exercises for more challenging and demanding roles that require hands-on learning, first-hand investigations, and the application of knowledge and thinking skills to complex problems.

The Schoolwide Enrichment Model (SEM) is a detailed blueprint for total school improvement that allows each school the flexibility to allow each school to develop its own unique programs based on local resources, student demographics, and school dynamics as well as faculty strengths and creativity. Although this research-based model is based on highly successful practices that originated in special programs for the gifted and talented students, its major goal is to promote both challenging and enjoyable high-end learning across a wide range of school types, levels and demographic differences. The idea is to create a repertoire of services that can be integrated in such a way to create "a rising tide lifts all ships" approach. This approach allows schools to develop a collaborative school culture that takes advantage of resources and appropriate decision-making opportunities to create meaningful, high-level and potentially creative opportunities for students to develop their talents. SEM suggests that educators should examine ways to make schools more inviting, friendly, and enjoyable places that encourage the full development of the learner instead of seeing students as a repository for information that will be assessed with the next round of stan-

---

[1] Research for this chapter was supported under the Javits Act Program (Grant No. R206R00001) as administered by the Office of Educational Research and Improvement, U.S. Department of Education. Grantees undertaking such projects are encouraged to express freely their professional judgment. This report, therefore, does not necessarily represent positions or policies of the Government, and no official, endorsement should be inferred.

[2] Reproduced from Renzulli, J. S. (n.d.). The schoolwide enrichment model executive summary. Retrieved June 9, 2004, from The University of Connecticut, Neag Center for Gifted Education and Talent Development web site: http://wwww.gifted.uconn.edu/semexec.html.

dardized tests. Not only has this model been successful in addressing the problem of students who have been under-challenged but it also provides additional important learning paths for students who find success in more traditional learning environments.

The present reform initiatives in general education have created a more receptive atmosphere for enrichment approaches that challenge all students, and accordingly, the Enrichment Triad Model has evolved over the last 20 years based on the previous experiences and current changes in general education. The evolution of the Enrichment Triad Model will be described in this chapter as well as the newest adaptation of the Schoolwide Enrichment Model including a description of the school structures upon which the model is targeted and the three service delivery components.

The original Enrichment Triad Model (Renzulli, 1976) was developed in the mid-1970s and initially implemented by school districts primarily in Connecticut in the United States. The model, which was originally field tested in several districts, proved to be quite popular and requests from all over the United States for visitations to schools using the model and for information about how to implement the model increased. A book about the Enrichment Triad Model (Renzulli, 1977) was published, and more and more districts began asking for help in implementing this approach. It was at this point that a clear need was established for research about the effectiveness of the model and for practical procedures that could provide technical assistance for interested educators to help develop programs in their schools. We had become fascinated by the various kinds of programs being developed by different types of teachers. In some programs, for example, teachers consistently elicited high levels of creative productivity in students while others had few students who engaged in this type of work. In some districts, many enrichment opportunities were regularly offered to students not formally identified for the program, while in other districts only identified 'gifted' students had access to enrichment experiences. We wondered how we could replicate the success of one teacher or one district in implementing the model. For example, if one teacher consistently produced high levels of creative productivity in students, how could we capture that technology and replicate it in other teachers? And if certain resources proved to be consequential in promoting desirable results, how could we make these resources available to larger numbers of teachers and students?

In the more than two decades since the Enrichment Triad Model has been used as the basis for many educational programs for gifted and talented students, an unusually large number of examples of creative productivity have occurred on the parts of young people whose educational experiences have been guided by this programming approach. Perhaps, like others involved in the development of theories and generalizations, we did not fully understand at the onset of our work the full implications of the model for encouraging and developing creative productivity in young people. These implications relate most directly to teacher training, resource procurement and management, product evaluation, and other theoretical concerns (e.g. motivation, task commitment, self-efficacy) that probably would have gone unexamined, undeveloped, and unrefined without the favorable results that were reported to us by early implementers of the model. We became increasingly interested in how and why the model was working and how we could further expand the theoretical rationale underlying our work, and the population to which services could be provided.

Thus, several years of conceptual analysis, practical experience, and an examination of the work of other theorists, has brought us to the point of tying together the material in this chapter, which represents approximately twenty years of field testing, research, evolution and dissemination.

In this chapter, an overview of the conception of giftedness upon which this model is based is presented, and a description of the original Enrichment Triad Model is provided as is a chronology of how the model has expanded and changed. Research about the model is presented as is a brief summary of research dealing with selected studies about student creative productivity. In the final section, new directions for the model are presented along with suggestions for future directions for research on creative productivity.

A Broadened Conception of Giftedness

The field of gifted education, like any other specialized area of study, represents a spectrum of ideologies that exists along a continuum ranging from conservative to liberal points of view. Conservative and liberal are not used here in their political connotations, but rather according to the degree of restrictiveness that is used in determining who is eligible for special programs and services.

Restrictiveness can be expressed in two ways; first, a definition can limit the number of specific performance areas that are considered in determining eligibility for special services. A conservative definition, for example, might limit eligibility to academic performance only and exclude other areas such as music, art, drama, leadership, public speaking, social service, creative writing or skills in interpersonal relations. Second, a definition can limit the degree or level of excellence that one must attain by establishing extremely high cutoff points.

Although liberal definitions have the obvious advantage of expanding the conception of giftedness, they also open up two theoretical concerns by introducing: (1) a values issue (How do we operationally define broader conceptions of giftedness?) and (2) the age-old problem of subjectivity in measurement. In recent years the values issue has been largely resolved. Very few educators cling tenaciously to a 'straight IQ' or purely academic definition of giftedness. 'Multiple talent' and 'multiple criteria' are almost the bywords of the present-day gifted education movement, and most people have little difficulty in, accepting a definition that includes most areas of human activity which are manifested in socially useful forms of expression.

The problem of subjectivity in measurement is not as easily resolved. As the definition of giftedness is extended beyond those abilities that are clearly reflected in tests of intelligence, achievement, and academic aptitude, it becomes necessary to put less emphasis on precise estimates of performance and potential and more emphasis on the opinions of qualified persons in making decisions about admission to special programs. The crux of the issue boils down to a simple and yet very important question: How much of a trade-off are we willing to make on the objective to subjective continuum in order to allow recognition of a broader spectrum of human abilities? If some degree of subjectivity cannot be tolerated, then our definitions of giftedness and the resulting programs will logically be limited to abilities that can be measured only by objective tests.

Two Kinds of Giftedness

It is generally accepted that intelligence is not a unitary concept, but rather there are many kinds of intelligence and therefore single definitions cannot be used to explain this multifaceted phenomenon (Neisser, 1979). The confusion and inconclusiveness about present theories of intelligence has led Sternberg (1984) and others to develop new models for explaining this complicated concept. Sternberg's 'triarchic' theory of human intelligence consists of three subtheories: a contextual subtheory, which relates intelligence to the external world of the individual; a two-facet experiential subtheory, which relates intelligence to both the external and internal worlds of the individual; and a componential subtheory, which relates intelligence to the internal world of the individual. Gardner (1983) proposed seven distinctive types of intelligent behavior which he called linguistic, logical-mathematical, spatial, bodily-kinesthetic, musical, interpersonal, intrapersonal, and the recently added naturalist intelligence.

In view of these recent works and numerous earlier cautions about the dangers of trying to describe intelligence through the use of single scores, it seems safe to conclude that this practice has been and always will be questionable. At the very least, attributes of intelligent behavior must be considered within the context of cultural and situational factors. Indeed, some of the most recent examinations have concluded that "[t]he concept of intelligence cannot be explicitly defined, not only because of the nature of intelligence but also because of the nature of concepts" (Neisser, 1979, p. 179).

There is no ideal way to measure intelligence and therefore we must avoid the typical practice of believing that if we know a person's IQ score, we also know his or her intelligence. Even Terman warned against total reliance on tests: "We must guard against defining intelligence solely in terms of ability to pass the tests of a given intelligence scale" (as cited in Thorndike, 1921, p. 131). E. L. Thorndike echoed Terman's concern by stating "to assume that we have measured some general power which resides in [the person being tested] and determines his ability in every variety of intellectual task in its entirety is to fly directly in the face of all that is known about the organization of the intellect" (Thorndike, 1921, p. 126).

The reason we have cited these concerns about the historical difficulty of defining and measuring intelligence is to highlight the even larger problem of isolating a unitary definition of giftedness. At the very least, we will always have several conceptions (and therefore definitions) of giftedness. To help in this analysis, we will begin by examining two broad categories of giftedness that have been dealt with in the research literature: 'schoolhouse giftedness' and 'creative-productive giftedness.' Before describing each type, we want to emphasize that:

1. Both types are important.
2. There is usually an interaction between the two types.
3. Special programs should make appropriate provisions for encouraging both types of giftedness as well as the numerous occasions when the two types interact with each other.

Schoolhouse Giftedness

Schoolhouse giftedness might also be called test-taking or lesson-learning giftedness. It is the kind most easily measured by IQ or other cognitive ability tests, and for this reason it is also the type most often used for selecting students for entrance into special programs. The abilities people display on IQ and aptitude tests are exactly the kinds of abilities most valued in traditional school learning situations. In other words, the tasks required in ability tests are similar in nature to tasks that teachers require in most lesson-learning situations. A large body of research tells us that students who score high on IQ tests are also likely to get high grades in school, and that these test-taking and lesson-learning abilities generally remain stable over time. The results of this research should lead us to some very obvious conclusions about schoolhouse giftedness: it exists in varying degrees, it can be identified through standardized assessment techniques, and we should therefore do everything in our power to make appropriate modifications for students who have the ability to cover regular curricular material at advanced rates and levels of understanding. Curriculum compacting (Renzulli, Smith, & Reis, 1982; Reis, Burns, & Renzulli, 1992) is a procedure used for modifying standard curricular content to accommodate advanced learners. Other acceleration techniques should represent essential parts of every school program that strives to respect the individual differences that are clearly evident from classroom performance and/or scores yielded by cognitive ability tests.

Creative-Productive Giftedness

If scores on IQ tests and other measures of cognitive ability only account for a limited proportion of the common variance with school grades, we can be equally certain that these measures do not tell the whole story when it comes to making predictions about creative-productive giftedness. Before defending this assertion with some research findings, we briefly review what is meant by this second type of giftedness, the important role that it should play in programming, and, therefore, the reasons we should attempt to assess it in our identification procedures—even if such assessment causes us to look below the top 3 to 5% on the normal curve of IQ scores.

Creative-productive giftedness. describes those aspects of human activity and involvement in which a premium is placed on the development of original material and products that are purposefully designed to have an impact on one or more target audiences. Learning situations that are designed to promote creative-productive giftedness emphasize the use and application of information (content) and thinking skills (process) in an integrated, inductive, and real-problem oriented manner. The role of the student is transformed from that of a learner of prescribed lessons to one in which she or he uses the modus operandi of a firsthand inquirer. This approach is quite different from the development of lesson-learning giftedness, which tends to emphasize deductive learning, structured training in the development of thinking processes, and the acquisition, storage, and retrieval of information. In other words, creative-productive giftedness is simply putting one's abilities to work on problems and areas of study that have personal relevance to the student and that can be escalated to appropriately challenging levels of investigative activity. The roles that both students and teachers should play in the pursuit of these problems have been described elsewhere

(Renzulli, 1977, 1982), and have been embraced in general education under a variety of concepts such as constructivist theory, authentic learning, discovery learning, problem based learning, and performance assessment.

Why is creative-productive giftedness important enough for us to question the "tidy" and relatively easy approach that has traditionally been used to select students on the basis of test scores? Why do some people want to rock the boat by challenging a conception of giftedness that can be numerically defined by simply giving a test? The answers to these questions are simple and yet very compelling. A review of the research literature (Renzulli, 1986) tells us that there is much more to identifying human potential than the abilities revealed on traditional tests of intelligence, aptitude, and achievement. Furthermore, history tells us it has been the creative and productive people of the world, the producers rather than consumers of knowledge, the reconstructionists of thought in all areas of human endeavor, who have become recognized as "truly gifted" individuals. History does not remember persons who merely scored well on IQ tests or those who learned their lessons well. The definition of giftedness (See Fig. 1) which characterizes creative productive giftedness and serves as part of the rationale for the Enrichment Triad Model is the three-ring conception of giftedness (Renzulli, 1978, 1986), in which giftedness:

> . . . consists of an interaction among three basic clusters being above average general ability, high levels of creativity. Gifted and talented capable of developing this composite set

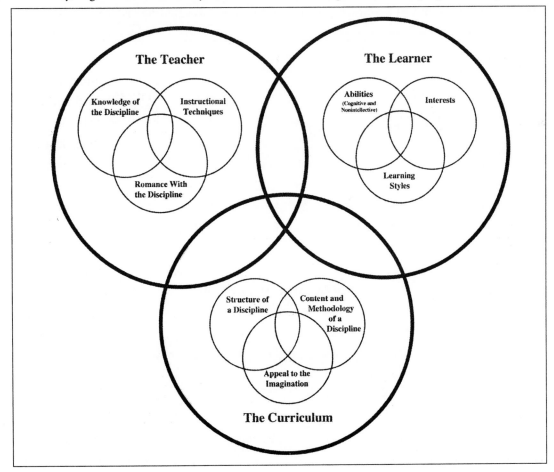

Figure 1. The three-ring conception of giftedness.

of potentially valuable area of human performance or capable of developing an interaction among these require a variety of educational opportunities and services those not normally through regular instructional programming. (1978, p. 6)

We have advocated that gifted behaviors can be developed through systematic enrichment opportunities described in the Enrichment Triad Model (Renzulli, 1977, 1978, 1988b).

An Overview of the Enrichment Triad Model

The Enrichment Triad Model was designed to encourage creative productivity on the part of young people by exposing them to various topics, areas of interest, and fields of study, and to further train them to apply advanced content, process-training skills, and methodology training to self-selected areas of interest. Accordingly, three types of enrichment are included in the Triad Model (see Fig. 2).

Type I enrichment is designed to expose students to a wide variety of disciplines, topics, occupations, hobbies, persons, places, and events that would not ordinarily be covered in the regular curriculum. In schools that use this model, an enrichment team consisting of parents, teachers, and students often organizes and plans Type I experiences by contacting speakers, arranging mini-courses, demonstrations, or performances, or by ordering and distributing films, slides, videotapes,

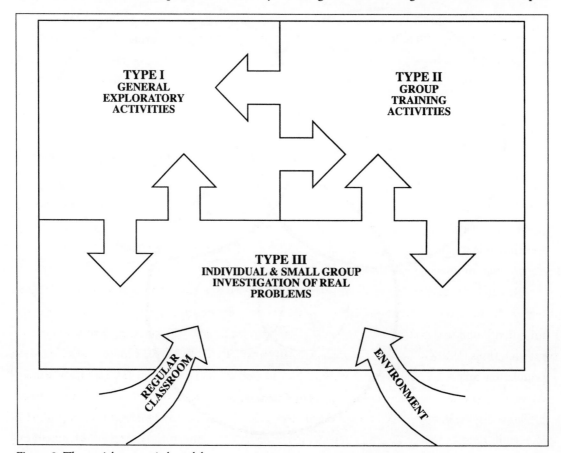

Figure 2. The enrichment triad model.

or other print or non-print media.

Type II enrichment consists of materials and methods designed to promote the development of thinking and feeling processes. Some Type II training is general, and is usually carried out both in classrooms and in enrichment programs. Training activities include the development of (1) creative thinking and problem solving, critical thinking, and affective processes; (2) a wide variety of specific learning how-to-learn skills; (3) skills in the appropriate use of advanced-level reference materials; and (4) written, oral, and visual communication skills. Other Type II enrichment is specific, as it cannot be planned in advance and usually involves advanced methodological instruction in an interest area selected by the student. For example, students who become interested in botany after a Type I experience might pursue additional training in this area by doing advanced reading in botany; compiling, planning and carrying out plant experiments; and seeking more advanced methods training if they want to go further.

Type III enrichment involves students who become interested in pursuing a self-selected area and are willing to commit the time necessary for advanced content acquisition and process training in which they assume the role of a first-hand inquirer. The goals of Type III enrichment include:

- providing opportunities for applying interests, knowledge, creative ideas and task commitment to a self-selected problem or area of study,
- acquiring advanced level understanding of the knowledge (content) and methodology (process) that are used within particular disciplines, artistic areas of expression and inter-disciplinary studies,
- developing authentic products that are primarily directed toward bringing about a desired impact upon a specified audience,
- developing self-directed learning skills in the areas of planning, organization, resource utilization, time management, decision making and self-evaluation,
- developing task commitment, self-confidence, and feelings of creative accomplishment.

The Revolving Door Identification Model

As our experience with Triad Programs grew, our concern about who was being identified to participate in these programs also grew. We became increasingly concerned about students who were not able to participate in enrichment programs because they did not score in the top 1-3% of the population in achievement or intelligence tests.

Research conducted by Torrance (1962, 1974) had demonstrated that students who were rated highly on creativity measures do well in school and on achievement tests but are often not selected for gifted programs because their scores are often below the cutoff for admission. Some of our own research (Reis, 1981) indicated that when a broader population of students (15-20% of the general population called the 'talent pool') were able to participate in Types I and II enrichment experiences, they produced equally good Type III products as the traditional 'gifted' students (the top 3-5%). This research produced the rationale for the Revolving Door Identification Model (RDIM) (Renzulli, Reis, & Smith, 1981) in which a talent pool of students receives regular enrichment experiences and the opportunity to 'revolve into' Type III creative productive experiences. In RDIM, we recommend that students be selected for participation in the talent pool on the basis of multiple criteria that include indices of creativity because we believe that one of the major purposes of gifted education is to develop creative thinking and creative productivity in students. Once identified and placed in the talent pool through the use of test scores; teacher, parent, or self-nomination; and examples of creative potential or productivity, students are observed in classrooms and enrichment experiences for signs of advanced interests, creativity, or task commitment. We have called this part of the process action information' and have found it to be an instrumental part of the identification process in assessing students' interest and motivation to become involved in Type III creative productivity. Further support for expanding identification procedures through the use of these approaches has recently been offered by Kirschenbaum (1983) and Kirschenbaum and Siegle (1993) who demonstrated that students who are rated or test high on measures of creativity tend to do well in school and on measures of achievement. The development of the RDIM led to the need for a guide dealing with how all of the components of the previous Triad and the new RDIM could be implemented and the resulting work was entitled *The Schoolwide Enrichment Model* (SEM) (Renzulli & Reis, 1985, 1997).

The Schoolwide Enrichment Model (SEM)

In the SEM, a talent pool of 15-20% of above average ability/high potential students is identified through a variety of measures including: achievement tests, teacher nominations, assessment of potential for creativity and task commitment, as well as alternative pathways of entrance (self-nomination, parent nomination, etc.). High achievement test and IQ test scores automatically include a student in the talent pool, enabling those students who are underachieving in their academic school work to be included.

Once students are identified for the talent pool, they are eligible for several kinds of services; first, interest and learning styles assessments are used with talent pool students. Informal and formal methods are used to create or identify students' interests and to encourage students to further develop and pursue these interests in various ways. Learning style preferences which are assessed include: projects, independent study, teaching games, simulations, peer teaching, programmed instruction, lecture, drill and recitation, and discussion. Second, curriculum compacting is provided to all eligible students for whom the regular curriculum is modified by eliminating portions of previously mastered content. This elimination or streamlining of curriculum enables above average students to avoid repetition of previously mastered work and guarantees mastery while simultaneously finding time for more appropriately challenging activities (Reis, Burns, & Renzulli, 1992; Renzulli, Smith & Reis, 1982). A form, entitled The Compactor (Renzulli & Smith, 1978), is used to document which content areas have been compacted and what alternative work has been substituted. Third, the Enrichment Triad Model, offers three types of enrichment experiences. Type I, II, and III Enrichment are offered to all students; however, Type III enrichment is usually more appropriate for students with higher levels of ability, interest, and task commitment.

Separate studies on the SEM demonstrated its effectiveness in schools with widely differing socioeconomic levels and program organization patterns (Olenchak, 1988; Olenchak & Renzulli, 1989). The SEM has been implemented in several hundred school districts across the country (Burns, 1998) and interest in this approach continues to grow.

Newest Directions for the Schoolwide Enrichment Model

The present reform initiatives in general education have created a more receptive atmosphere for more flexible approaches that challenge all students, and accordingly, the Schoolwide Enrichment Model (SEM) has been expanded to address three major goals that we believe will accommodate the needs of gifted students, and at the same time, provide challenging learning experiences for all students. These goals are:

- To maintain and expand a continuum of special services that will challenge students with demonstrated superior performance or the potential for superior performance in any and all aspects of the school and extracurricular program.
- To infuse into the general education program a broad range of activities for high-end learning that will (a) challenge all students to perform at advanced levels and (b) that will allow teachers to determine which students should be given extended opportunities, resources, and encouragement in particular areas where superior interest and performance are demonstrated.
- To preserve and protect the positions of gifted education specialists and any other specialized personnel necessary for carrying out the first two goals.

A graphic representation of the newest adaptation of the model is presented in Fig. 3.

School Structures

The Regular Curriculum

The regular curriculum consists of everything that is a part of the predetermined goals, schedules, learning outcomes, and delivery systems of the school. The regular curriculum might be traditional, innovative, or in the process of transition, but its predominant feature is that authoritative forces (i.e. policy makers, school councils, textbook adoption committees, state regulators) have determined that the regular curriculum should be the 'centerpiece' of student learning. Application of the SEM influences the regular curriculum in three ways. First, the challenge level of required material is differentiated through processes such as curriculum compacting and textbook content modification procedures. Second, systematic content intensification procedures should be used to replace eliminated content with selected, in-depth learning experiences. Third, types of enrichment recommended in the Enrichment Triad Model (Renzulli, 1977) are integrated selectively into regular curriculum activities. Although our goal in the SEM is to influence rather than replace the regular curriculum, application of certain SEM components and related staff development activities has resulted in substantial changes in both the content and instructional processes of the entire regular curriculum.

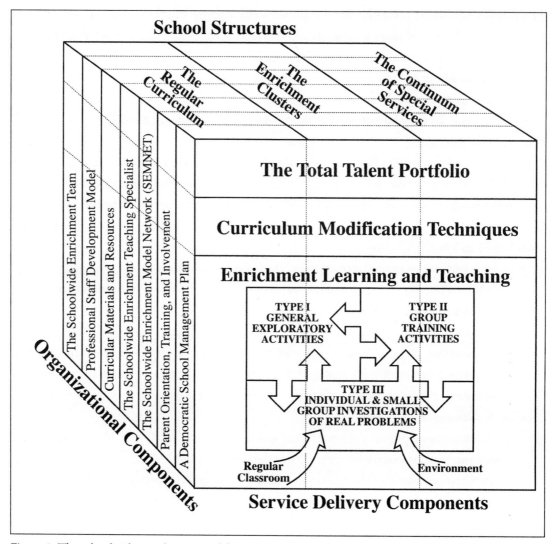

Figure 3. The schoolwide enrichment model.

The Enrichment Clusters

The enrichment clusters, one component of the Schoolwide Enrichment Model, are non-graded groups of students who share common interests, and who come together during specially designated time blocks during school to work with an adult who shares their interests and who has some degree of advanced knowledge and expertise in the area. The enrichment clusters usually meet for a block of time weekly during a semester. All students complete an interest inventory developed to assess their interests, and an enrichment team of parents and teachers tally all of the major families of interests. Adults from the faculty, staff, parents, and community are recruited to facilitate enrichment clusters based on these interests, such as creative writing, drawing, sculpting, archeology and other areas. Training is provided to the facilitators who agree to offer the clusters, and a brochure is developed and sent to all parents and students that discusses student interests and select choices of enrichment clusters. A title and description that appeared in a brochure of clusters in a school using the SEM follows:

Invention Convention

Are you an inventive thinker? Would you like to be? Brainstorm a problem, try to identify many solutions, and design an invention to solve the problem, as an inventor might give birth to a real invention. Create your invention individually or with a partner under the guidance of Bob Erikson and his students, who work at the Connecticut Science Fair. You may share your final product at the Young Inventors' Fair on March 25th, a statewide daylong celebration of creativity.

Students select their top three choices for the clusters and scheduling is completed to place all children into their first, or in some cases, second choice. Like extracurricular activities and programs such as 4-H and Junior Achievement, the main rationale for participation in one or more clusters is that students and teachers want to be there. All teachers (including music, art, physical education, etc.) are involved in teaching the clusters; and their involvement in any particular cluster is based on the same type of interest assessment that is used for students in selecting clusters of choice.

The model for learning used with enrichment clusters is based on an inductive approach to solving real-world problems through the development of authentic products and services. Unlike traditional, didactic modes of teaching, this approach, known as enrichment learning and teaching (described fully in a later section), uses the Enrichment Triad Model to create a learning situation that involves the use of methodology, develops higher order thinking skills, and authentically applies these skills in creative and productive situations. Enrichment clusters promote cooperativeness within the context of real-world problem solving, and they also provide superlative opportunities for promoting self-concept. "A major assumption underlying the use of enrichment clusters is that every child is special if we create conditions in which that child can be a specialist within a specialty group" (Renzulli, 1994, p. 70).

Enrichment clusters are organized around various characteristics of differentiated programming for gifted students on which the Enrichment Triad Model (Renzulli, 1977) was originally based, including the use of major disciplines, interdisciplinary themes, or cross-disciplinary topics (e.g. a theatrical/television production group that includes actors, writers, technical specialists, costume designers). The clusters are modeled after the ways in which knowledge utilization, thinking skills, and interpersonal relations take place in the real world. Thus, all work is directed toward the production of a product or service. No lesson plans or unit plans are created in advance by the cluster facilitator; rather, direction is provided by three key questions addressed in the cluster by the facilitator and the students:

1. What do people with an interest in this area (e.g. film making) do?
2. What knowledge, materials, and other resources do they need to do it in an excellent and authentic way?
3. In what ways can the product or service be used to have an impact on an intended audience?

Enrichment clusters incorporate the use of advanced content, providing students with information about particular fields of knowledge, such as the structure of a field as well as the basic principles and the functional concepts in a field (Ward, 1960). Ward defined functional concepts as the intellectual instruments or tools with which a subject specialist works, such as the vocabulary of a field and the vehicles by which persons within the field communicate with one another. The methodology used within a field is also considered advanced content by Renzulli (1988a), involving the use of knowledge of the structures and tools of fields, as well as knowledge about the methodology of particular fields. This knowledge about the methodologies of fields exists both for the sake of increased knowledge acquisition, and also for the utility of that know-how as applied to the development of products, even when such products are considered advanced in a relative sense (i.e. age, grade, and background considerations).

The enrichment clusters are not intended to be the total program for talent development in a school, or to replace existing programs for talented youth. Rather, they are one vehicle for stimulating interests and developing talent potentials across the entire school population. They are also vehicles for staff development in that they provide teachers an opportunity to participate in enrichment teaching, and subsequently to analyze and compare this type of teaching with traditional methods of instruction. In this regard the model promotes a spill-over effect by encouraging teachers to become better talent scouts and talent developers, and to apply enrichment techniques to regular classroom situations.

The Continuum of Special Services

A broad range of special services is the third school structure targeted by the model; a diagram representing these services is presented in Fig. 4. Although the enrichment clusters and the SEM-based modifications of the regular curriculum provide a broad range of services to meet individual needs, a program for total talent development still requires supplementary services that challenge young people who are capable of working at the highest levels of their special interest and ability areas. These services, which cannot ordinarily be provided in enrichment clusters or the regular curriculum, typically include: individual or small group counseling, direct assistance in facilitating advanced level work, arranging for mentorships with faculty members or community persons, and making other types of connections between students, their families, and out-of-school persons, resources, and agencies.

Direct assistance also involves setting up and promoting student, faculty and parental involvement in special programs such as Future Problem Solving, Odyssey of the Mind, the Model United Nations program, and state and national essay, mathematics, art, and history contests. Another type of direct assistance consists of arranging out-of-school involvement for individual students in summer programs, on-campus courses, special schools, theatrical groups, scientific expeditions, and apprenticeships at places where advanced level learning opportunities are available. Provision of these services is one of the responsibilities of the schoolwide enrichment teaching specialist or an enrichment team of teachers and parents who work together to provide options for advanced learning. A schoolwide enrichment teaching specialist in Barrington, Rhode Island, estimates she spends two days a week in a resource capacity to the faculties of two schools, and

104

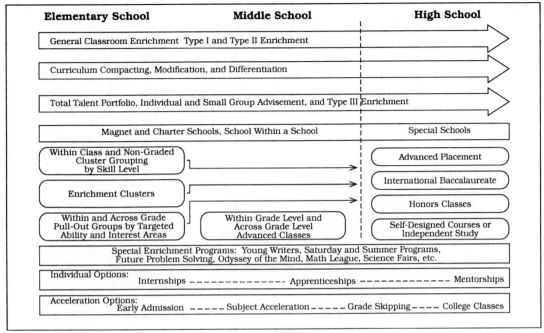

Figure 4. The continuum of services for total talent development.

three days providing direct services to students.

Service Delivery Components

The Total Talent Portfolio

The Schoolwide Enrichment Model targets specific learning characteristics that can serve as a basis for talent development. Our approach to targeting learning characteristics uses both traditional and performance-based assessment to compile information about three dimensions of the learner—abilities, interests, and learning styles. This information, which focuses on strengths rather than deficits, is compiled in a management form called the 'Total Talent Portfolio' (see Fig. 5) which is used to make decisions about talent development opportunities in regular classes, enrichment clusters, and in the continuum of special services. The major purposes of the Total Talent Portfolio are:

1. To *collect* several different types of information that portray a student's strength areas, and to regularly update this information.

2. To *classify* this information into the general categories of abilities, interests, and learning styles and related markers of successful learning such as organizational skills, content area preferences, personal and social skills, preferences for creative productivity, and learning-how-to-learn skills.

3. To periodically *review and analyze* the information in order to make purposeful decisions about providing opportunities for enrichment experiences in the regular classroom, the enrichment clusters, and the continuum of special services.

4. To *negotiate* various acceleration and enrichment learning options and opportunities be-

105

Joseph S. Renzulli

Abilities	Interests	Style Preferences			
Maximum Performance Indicators	*Interest Areas*	*Instructional Styles Preferences*	*Learning Environment Preferences*	*Thinking Styles Preferences*	*Expression Style Preferences*
Tests	Fine Arts	Recitation & Drill		Analytic	Written
•Standardized	Crafts	Peer Tutoring	*Inter/Intra Personal*	(School Smart)	
•Teacher-Made	Literary	Lecture	•Self-Oriented		Oral
Course Grades	Historical	Lecture/Discussion	•Peer-Oriented	Synthetic/	
Teacher Ratings	Mathematical/Logical	Discussion	•Adult-Oriented	Creative	Manipulative
Product Evaluation	Physical Sciences	Guided Independent	•Combined	(Creative, Inventive)	
•Written	Life Sciences	Study *			Discussion
•Oral	Political/Judicial	Learning /Interest Center	*Physical*	Practical/	
•Visual	Athletic/Recreation	Simulation, Role Playing,	•Sound	Contextual	Display
•Musical	Marketing/Business	Dramatization, Guided Fantasy	•Heat	(Street Smart)	
•Constructed	Drama/Dance	Learning Games	•Light		Dramatization
(Note differences between assigned and self-selected products)	Musical Performance	Replicative Reports or Projects*	•Design	Legislative	Artistic
Level of Participation in Learning Activities	Musical Composition	Investigative Reports or Projects*	•Mobility	Executive	Graphic
	Managerial/Business	Unguided Independent Study*	•Time of Day		
Degree of Interaction With Others	Photography	Internship*	•Food Intake	Judicial	Commercial
	Film/Video	Apprenticeship*	•Seating		Service
	Computers			Ref: Sternberg, 1984, 1988, 1990	
Ref: General Tests and Measurements Literature	Other (Specify)	*With or without a mentor	Ref: Amabile, 1983; Dunn, Dunn, & Price, 1977; Gardner, 1983		Ref: Kettle, Renzulli, & Rizza, 1998; Renzulli & Reis, 1985
	Ref: Renzulli, 1997	Ref: Renzulli & Smith, 1978			

Figure 5. The total talent portfolio.

tween teacher and student through participation in a shared decision making process.

5. To *use the information* as a vehicle for educational, personal, and career counseling and for communicating with parents about the school's talent development opportunities and their child's involvement in them.

This expanded approach to identifying talent potentials is essential if we are to make genuine efforts to include more under-represented students in a plan for total talent development. This approach is also consistent with the more flexible conception of developing gifts and talents that has been a cornerstone of our work and our concerns for promoting more equity in special programs.

Curriculum Modification Techniques

The second service delivery component of the SEM is a series of curriculum modification techniques designed to: (1) adjust levels of required learning so that all students are challenged, (2) increase the number of in-depth learning experiences, and (3) introduce various types of enrichment into regular curricular experiences. The procedures that are used to carry out curriculum modification are curriculum compacting, textbook analysis and surgical removal of repetitious material from textbooks, and a planned approach for introducing greater depth into regular curricular material. Due to space restrictions, curriculum compacting is described in depth here and other modification techniques are described in detail in other publications (see, for example, Renzulli, 1994; Reis et al., 1993).

How to Use the Compacting Process

Defining goals and outcomes. The first of three phases of the compacting process consists of defining the goals and outcomes of a given unit or segment of instruction. This information is readily available in most subjects because specific goals and outcomes can usually be found in teachers' manuals, curriculum guides, scope-and-sequence charts, and some of the new curricular frameworks that are emerging in connection with outcome-based education models. Teachers should examine these objectives to determine which represent the acquisition of new content or thinking skills as opposed to reviews or practice of material that has previously been taught. The scope and sequence charts prepared by publishers, or a simple comparison of the table of contents of a basal series will provide a quick overview of new vs. repeated material. A major goal of this phase of the compacting process is to help teachers make individual programming decisions; a larger professional development goal is to help teachers be better analysts of the material they are teaching and better consumers of textbooks and prescribed curricular material.

Identifying students for compacting. The second phase of curriculum compacting is identifying students who have already mastered the objectives or outcomes of a unit or segment of instruction that is about to be taught. This first step of this phase consists of estimating which students have the potential to master new material at a faster than normal pace; knowing one's students is, of course, the best way to begin the assessment process. Scores on previous tests, completed assignments, and classroom participation are the best ways of identifying highly likely candidates for compacting. Standardized achievement tests can serve as a good general screen for this step because they allow us to list the names of all students who are scoring one or more years above grade level in particular subject areas.

Being a candidate for compacting does not necessarily mean that a student knows the material under consideration. Therefore, the second step of identifying candidates consists of finding or developing appropriate tests or other assessment techniques that can be used to evaluate specific learning outcomes. Unit pretests or end-of-unit tests that can be administered as pretests are ready-made for this task, especially when it comes to the assessment of basic skills. An analysis of pretest results enables the teacher to document proficiency in specific skills, and to select instructional activities or practice material necessary to bring the student up to a high level on any skill that may need some additional reinforcement.

The process is slightly modified for compacting content areas that are not as easily assessed as basic skills, and for students who have not mastered the material, but are judged to be candidates for more rapid coverage. First, students should have a thorough understanding of the goals and procedures of compacting, including the nature of the replacement process. A given segment of material should be discussed with the student (e.g. a unit that includes a series of chapters in a social studies text), and the procedures for verifying mastery at a high level should be specified. These procedures might consist of answering questions based on the chapters, writing an essay, or taking the standard end-of-unit test. The amount of time for completion of the unit should be specified, and procedures such as periodic progress reports or log entries for teacher review should be agreed upon. Of course, an examination of potential acceleration and/or enrichment replacement activities should be a part of this discussion.

Another alternative is to assess or pretest all students in a class when a new unit or topic is introduced; although this may seem like more work for the teacher, it provides the opportunity for all students to demonstrate their strengths or previous mastery in a given area. Using a matrix of learning objectives, teachers can fill in test results and establish small, flexible, and temporary groups for skill instruction and replacement activities.

Providing acceleration and enrichment options. The final phase of the compacting process can be one of the most exciting aspects of teaching because it is based on cooperative decision making and creativity on the parts of both teachers and students. Efforts can be made to gather enrichment materials from classroom teachers, librarians, media specialists, and content area or gifted education specialists. These materials may include self-directed learning activities, instructional materials that focus on particular thinking skills, and a variety of individual and group project oriented activities that are designed to promote hands-on research and investigative skills. The time made available through compacting provides opportunities for exciting learning experiences such as small group, special topic seminars that might be directed by students or community resource persons, community based apprenticeships or opportunities to work with a mentor, peer tutoring situations, involvement in community service activities, and opportunities to rotate through a series of self-selected mini-courses. The time saved through curriculum compacting can be used by the teacher to provide a variety of enrichment or acceleration opportunities for the student.

Enrichment strategies might include a variety of Type I, II, or III [activities] or a number of options included on the continuum of services. Acceleration might include the use of material from the next unit or chapter, the use of the next chronological grade level textbook, or the completion of even more advanced work. Alternative activities should reflect an appropriate level of challenge and rigor that is commensurate with the student's abilities and interests.

Decisions about which replacement activities to use are always guided by factors such as time, space, and the availability of resource persons and materials. Although practical concerns must be considered, the ultimate criteria for replacement activities should be the degree to which they increase academic challenge and the extent to which they meet individual needs. Great care should be taken to select activities and experiences that represent individual strengths and interests rather than the assignment of more-of-the-same worksheets or randomly selected kits, games, and puzzles! This aspect of the compacting process should also be viewed as a creative opportunity for an entire faculty to work cooperatively to organize and institute a broad array of enrichment experiences. A favorite mini-course that a faculty member has always wanted to teach or serving as a mentor to one or two students who are extremely invested in a teacher's beloved topic are just a few of the ways that replacement activities can add excitement to the teachers' part in this process as well as the obvious benefits for students. We have also observed another interesting occurrence that has resulted from the availability of curriculum compacting. When some previously bright but under-achieving students realized that they could both economize on regularly assigned material and 'earn time' to pursue self-selected interests, their motivation to complete regular assignments increased; as one student put it, "Everyone understands a good deal!"

The best way to get an overview of the curriculum compacting process is to examine an actual example of how the management form that guides this process is used. This form, 'The Compactor,' presented in Fig. 6, serves as both an organizational and record keeping tool. Teachers should fill out one form per student, or one form for a group of students with similar curricular strengths. Completed Compactors should be kept in students' academic files, and updated on a regular basis. The form can also be used for small groups of students who are working at approximately the same level (e.g. a reading or math group). The Compactor is divided into three sections:

- The first column should include information on learning objectives and student strengths in those areas. Teachers should list the objectives for a particular unit of study, followed by data on students' proficiency in those objectives, including test scores, behavioral profiles and past academic records.
- In the second column, teachers should detail the pretest vehicles they select, along with test results. The pretest instruments can be formal measures, such as pencil and paper tests, or informal measures, such as performance assessments based on observations of class participation and written assignments. Specificity is extremely important; recording an overall score of 85% on ten objectives, for example, sheds little light on what portion of the material can be compacted, since students might show limited mastery of some objectives and high levels of mastery on others.
- Column three is used to record information about acceleration or enrichment options; in determining these options, teachers must be fully aware of students' individual interests and learning styles. We should never replace compacted regular curriculum work with harder, more advanced material that is solely determined by the teacher; instead, students interests

INDIVIDUAL EDUCATIONAL PROGRAMMING GUIDE
The Compactor

Prepared by: Joseph S. Renzulli
Linda M. Smith

NAME__________ AGE_____ TEACHER(S)__________ Individual Conference Dates And Persons Participating in Planning Of IEP

SCHOOL__________ GRADE_____ PARENT(S)__________

CURRICULUM AREAS TO BE CONSIDERED FOR COMPACTING Provide a brief description of basic material to be covered during this marking period and the assessment information or evidence that suggests the need for compacting.	PROCEDURES FOR COMPACTING BASIC MATERIAL Describe activities that will be used to guarantee proficiency in basic curricular areas.	ACCELERATION AND/OR ENRICHMENT ACTIVITIES Describe activities that will be used to provide advanced level learning experiences in each area of the regular curriculum.

☐ Check here if additional information is recorded on the reverse side.

Figure 6. The compactor.

should be taken, into account. If for example, a student loves working on science fair projects, that option may be used to replace material that has been compacted from the regular curriculum. We should also be careful to help monitor the challenge level of the material that is being substituted. We want students to understand the nature of effort and challenge and we should ensure that students are not simply replacing the compacted material with basic reading or work that is not advanced.

Rosa: A Case Study in Curriculum Compacting

Rosa is a fifth grader in a self-contained heterogeneous classroom; her school is located in a lower socio-economic urban school district. While Rosa's reading and language scores range between four or five years above grade level, most of her 29 classmates are reading one to two years below grade. level. This presented Rosa's teacher with a common problem: what was the best way to instruct Rosa? He agreed to compact her curriculum. Taking the easiest approach possible, he administered all of the appropriate unit tests for the grade level in the Basal Language Arts program, and excused Rosa from completing the activities and worksheets in the units where she showed proficiency (80% and above). When Rosa missed one or two questions, the teacher checked for trends in those items and provided instruction and practice materials to ensure concept mastery.

Rosa usually took part in language arts lessons one or two days a week; the balance of the time she spent with alternative projects, some of which she selected. This strategy spared Rosa up to six or eight hours a week with language arts skills that were simply beneath her level. She joined the class instruction only when her pretests indicated she had not fully acquired the skills or to take part in a discussion that her teacher thought she would enjoy. In the time saved through compacting, Rosa engaged in a number of enrichment activities. First, she spent as many as five hours a week in a resource room for high ability students. This time was usually scheduled during her language arts class, benefiting both Rosa and her teacher, since he didn't have to search for all of the enrichment options himself. The best part of the process for Rosa was she didn't have make-up regular classroom assignments because she was not missing essential work.

Rosa also visited a regional science center with other students who had expressed a high interest and aptitude for science. Science was a second strength area for Rosa, and based on the results of her Interest-A-Lyzer, a decision was made for Rosa to proceed with a science fair project on growing plants under various conditions. Rosa's Compactor, which covered an entire semester, was updated in January. Her teacher remarked that compacting her curriculum had actually saved him time—time he would have spent correcting papers needlessly assigned! The value of compacting for Rosa convinced him that he should continue the process. The Compactor was also used as a vehicle for explaining to Rosa's parents how specific modifications were being made to accommodate her advanced language arts achievement level and her interest in science. A copy of The Compactor was also passed on to Rosa's sixth grade teacher, and a conference between the fifth and sixth grade teachers and the resource teacher helped to ensure continuity in dealing with Rosa's special needs.

The many changes that are taking place in our schools require all educators to examine a broad range of techniques for providing equitably for all students. Curriculum compacting is one such process. It is not tied to a specific content area or grade level, nor is it aligned with a particular approach to school or curricular reform. Rather, the process is adaptable to any school configuration or curricular framework, and it is flexible enough to be used within the context of rapidly changing approaches to general education. The research study described above, and practical experience gained through several years of field testing and refining the compacting process have demonstrated that many positive benefits can result from this process for both students and teachers.

Enrichment Learning and Teaching

The third service delivery component of the SEM, which is based on the Enrichment Triad Model, is enrichment learning and teaching which has roots in the ideas of a small but influential number of philosophers, theorists, and researchers such as Jean Piaget (1975), Jerome Bruner (1960, 1966), and John Dewey (1913, 1916). The work of these theorists coupled with our own research and program development activities, has given rise to the concept we call enrichment learning and teaching. The best way to define this concept is in terms of the following four principles:

1. Each learner is unique, and therefore, all learning experiences must be examined in ways that take into account the abilities, interests, and learning styles of the individual.

2. Learning is more effective when students enjoy what they are doing, and therefore, learning experiences should be constructed and assessed with as much concern for enjoyment as for other goals.

3. Learning is more meaningful and enjoyable when content (i.e. knowledge) and process (i.e. thinking skills, methods of inquiry) are learned within the context of a real and present problem; and therefore, attention should be given to opportunities to personalize student choice in problem selection, the relevance of the problem for individual students at the time the problem is being addressed, and authentic strategies for addressing the problem.

4. Some formal instruction may be used in enrichment learning and teaching, but a major goal of this approach to learning is to enhance knowledge and thinking skill acquisition that is gained through formal instruction with applications of knowledge and skills that result from students' own construction of meaning (Renzulli, 1994, p. 204).

The ultimate goal of learning that is guided by these principles is to replace dependent and passive learning with independence and engaged learning. Although all but the most conservative educators will agree with these principles, much controversy exists about how these (or similar) principles might be applied in everyday school situations. A danger also exists that these principles might be viewed as yet another idealized list of glittering generalities that cannot be manifested easily in schools that are entrenched in the deductive model of learning; developing a school program based on these principles is not an easy task. Over the years, however, we have achieved success by gaining faculty, administrative, and parental consensus on a small number of easy-to-understand concepts and related services, and by providing resources and training related to each concept and service delivery procedure. Numerous research studies and field tests in schools with widely varying demographics have been carried out (Renzulli & Reis, 1994). These studies and field tests provided opportunities for the development of large amounts of practical know-how that are readily available for schools that would like to implement the SEM. They also have shown that the SEM can be implemented in a wide variety of settings and used with various populations of students including high ability students with learning disabilities and high ability students who underachieve in school.

References

Amabile, T. (1983). *The social psychology of creativity*. New York. Springer-Verlag.

Bruner, J. S. (1960). *The process of education*. Cambridge, MA: Harvard University Press.

Bruner, J. S. (1966). *Toward a theory of instruction*. Cambridge, MA: Harvard University Press.

Burns, D. E. (1998). *SEM network directory*. Storrs, CT: University of Connecticut, Neag Center for Gifted Education and Talent Development.

Dewey, J. (1913). *Interest and effort in education*. New York: Houghton Mifflin.

Dewey, J. (1916). *Democracy and education*. New York: Macmillan.

Dunn, R., Dunn, K., & Price, G. E. (1977). Diagnosing learning styles: Avoiding malpractice suits against school systems. *Phi Delta Kappan, 58*(5), 418-420.

Gardner, H. (1983). *Frames of mind*. New York: Basic Books.

James, W. (1885). On the functions of cognition. *Mind, 10*, 27-44.

Kirschenbaum, R. J. (1983). Let's cut out the cut-off score in the identification of the gifted. *Roeper Review: A Journal on Gifted Education, 5*, 6-10.

Kirschenbaum, R. J. & Siegle, D. (1993, April). *Predicting creative performance in an enrichment program*. Paper presented at the Association for the Education of Gifted Underachieving Students 6th Annual Conference, Portland, OR.

Neisser, U. (1979). The concept of intelligence. In R. J. Sternberg & D. K. Detterman (Eds.), *Human Intelligence* (pp. 179-189). Norwood, NJ: Ablex.

Olenchak, F. R. (1988). The schoolwide enrichment model in the elementary schools: A study of implementation stages and effects on educational excellence. In: J. S. Renzulli (Ed.), *Technical Report on Research Studies Relating to the Revolving Door Identification Model* (2nd ed., pp. 201-247). Storrs, CT: University of Connecticut, Bureau of Educational Research.

Olenchak, F R. & Renzulli, J. S. (1989). The effectiveness of the schoolwide enrichment model on selected aspects of elementary school change. *Gifted Child Quarterly, 32*, 44-57.

Piaget, J. (1975). *The development of thought: Equilibration on of cognitive structures*. New York: Viking.

Reis, S. M. (1981). *An analysis of the productivity of gifted students participating in programs using the revolving door identification model*. Unpublished doctoral dissertation, University of Connecticut, Storrs.

Reis, S. M., Burns, D. E. & Renzulli, J. S. (1992). *Curriculum compacting: The complete guide to modifying the regular curriculum for high ability students*. Mansfield Center, CT: Creative Learning Press.

Reis, S. M., Westberg, K. L., Kulikowich, J., Caillard, F., Hébert, T. P., Plucker, J. A., Purcell, J.

H., Rogers, J. & Smist, J. (1993). *Why not let high ability students start school in January? The curriculum compacting study* (Research Monograph 93106). Storrs, CT: University of Connecticut, The National Research Center on the Gifted and Talented.

Renzulli, J. S. (1976). The enrichment triad model: A guide for developing defensible programs for the gifted and talented. *Gifted Child Quarterly, 20,* 303-326.

Renzulli, J. S. (1977). *The enrichment triad model: A guide for developing defensible programs for the gifted and talented.* Mansfield Center, CT: Creative Learning Press.

Renzulli, J. S. (1978). What makes giftedness? Re-examining a definition. *Phi Delta Kappan, 60,* 180-184, 261.

Renzulli, J. S. (1982). What makes a problem real: Stalking the illusive meaning of qualitative differences in gifted education. *Gifted Child Quarterly, 26,* 147-156.

Renzulli, J. S. (1986). The three ring conception of giftedness: A developmental model for creative productivity. In R. J. Sternberg & J. E. Davidson (Eds.), *Conceptions of giftedness* (pp. 53-92). New York: Cambridge University Press.

Renzulli, J. S. (1988a). The multiple menu model for developing differentiated curriculum for the gifted and talented. *Gifted Child Quarterly, 32,* 298-309.

Renzulli, J. S. (Ed.). (1988b). *Technical report of research studies related to the enrichment triad/revolving door model* (3rd ed.). Storrs, CT: University of Connecticut, Teaching The Talented Program.

Renzulli, J. S. (1994). *Schools for talent development: A practical plan for total school improvement.* Mansfield Center, CT: Creative Learning Press.

Renzulli, J. S. & Reis, S. M. (1985). *The schoolwide enrichment model: A comprehensive plan for educational excellence.* Mansfield Center, CT: Creative Learning Press.

Renzulli, J. S. & Reis, S. M. (1994). Research related to the Schoolwide Enrichment Model. *Gifted Child Quarterly, 38,* 2-14.

Renzulli, J. S. & Reis, S. M. (1997). *The schoolwide enrichment model: A how-to guide for educational excellence.* Mansfield Center, CT: Creative Learning Press.

Renzulli, J. S., Reis, S. M., & Smith, L. H. (1981). *The revolving door identification model.* Mansfield Center, CT: Creative Learning Press.

Renzulli, J. S. & Smith, L. H. (1978). *The compactor.* Mansfield Center, CT: Creative Learning Press.

Renzulli, J. S., Smith, L. H. & Reis, S. M. (1982). Curriculum compacting: An essential strategy for working with gifted students. *The Elementary School Journal, 82,* 185-194.

Sternberg, R. J. (1984). Toward a triarchic theory of human intelligence. *Behavioral and Brain Sciences, 7,* 269-287.

Sternberg, R. J. (1988). Three facet model of creativity. In R. J. Sternberg (Ed.), *The Nature of Creativity* (pp. 125-147). Boston: Cambridge University Press.

Sternberg, R. J. (1990). Thinking styles: Keys to understanding student performance. *Phi Delta Kappan, 71(5),* 366-371.

Thorndike, E. L. (1921). Intelligence and its measurement. *Journal of Educational Psychology, 12,*

124-127.

Torrance, E. P. (1962). *Guiding creative talent.* Englewood Cliffs, NJ: Prentice-Hall.

Torrance, E. P. (1974). *Norms-Technical manual: Torrance tests of creative thinking.* Bensenville, IL: Scholastic Testing Service.

Ward, V. S. (1960). Systematic intensification and extensification of the school curriculum. *Exceptional Children, 28,* 67-71,77.

APPENDIX B: SAMPLE DOCUMENTS

PROFESSIONAL DEVELOPMENT PLAN
Webster Schools Schoolwide Enrichment Model Long Range Program Plan*
Stage 1: Preparation—Program Development & Start Up

KEY ACTIVITY	RESP. PARTIES	STATUS	DELIVERABLES
	District Office		
1. Commit enrichment model to priority level	Super.	Completed	Commitment statement, publicity
2. Develop long range plan with principals, staff development office, community relations, GATES	ASCI	Completed	Project plan
3. Determine personnel needs	ASCI	Completed	Staffing plan
4. Allocate funds	Super.	Completed	Budget
5. Develop organization, function of key players (DPS, staff development office, principals, enrichment coordinator, coaches, steering committee)	ASCI	Completed	Organization chart w/ function description
6. Develop criteria, job description for enrichment coordinator, ES	ASCI	Completed	Job descriptions
7. Develop profile, criteria for advisory committee membership, recruitment process	ASCI	Completed	Consensus documents
8. Develop CAC charter	ASCI	Completed	Charter document
9. Convene CAC committee	ASCI, Super.	Completed	Charter, processes and agenda
10. Identify ES leader and assign role	ASCI, Super.	Completed	Candidate roles and expectations
11. Develop staff development plan for enrichment specialists	ES Team	Completed	Initial staff development objectives & plan
12. Design metric for classroom differentiation	Consultant	In Process	Metric
13. Define curriculum development integration process	ASCI	In Process	Approach & framework for plan
14. Develop K-12 districtwide reporting system	DPD	In Process	Report cards

Abbreviations: AIS (Academic Intervention Service), **ASCI** (Assistant Superintendent for Curriculum and Instruction), **BOE** (Board of Education), **CAC** (Community Advisory Committee), **CCC** (Computer Curriculum Corp.), **CMS** (Curriculum Management System), **CPE** (Community Partnerships for Enrichment), **DCR** (Director of Community Relations), **DDM** (Director of Data Management), **DPD** (Director of Professional Development), **DPS** (Director of Pupil Services), **ES** (Enrichment Specialist), **GATES** (Gifted and Talented Education Supporters), **GS** (Grading System), **PPC** (Professional Practices Committee), **P/T** (Parent/Teacher), **RC** (Report Card), **RFP** (Request for Proposal), **Super.** (Superintendent), **UVA** (University of Virginia)

*Developed by Ellen Agostinelli, Webster Central School District, Webster, NY. Used with permission.

KEY ACTIVITY	RESP. PARTIES	STATUS	DELIVERABLES
15. Develop districtwide assessment/rubric system	DPD	In Process	Assessments per grade, unit
16. Develop K-12 districtwide testing program	AIS	In Process	Lists of tests per grade
17. Develop & roll-out initial program communication plan	Community Relations	Completed	Plan, content, mediums & schedules
18. Establish school-based program planning frameworks	ASCI/Principals	In Process	Consensus frameworks & process
19. Update BOE as per program progress	ES Team	Ongoing	Presentation to BOE
20. Develop districtwide referral process with principals	ES Team	Completed	Defined expectations and process
Schools			
1. Hire enrichment specialist	Site Team	Completed	Recommendation for hire form
2. Present program intent, highlights to faculty	Principal(s)	Completed	Agenda
3. Establish building team	Principal(s)	Completed	Membership list
4. Plan staff development for team, full faculty	Principal(s)	Completed	Program, schedule, and attendance
5. Develop school proposal with initial differentiation goals	Site Team	Completed	Initial start-up plan
6. Share plan with staff	Site Team	Completed	Agenda & process
7. Share proposal with ASCI for consistency & adaptation	Principal(s)	Completed	Approved plan
8. Share completed plan with staff	Principal(s)	Completed	Agenda

Stage II: Implementation—Phase I: Differentiation

KEY ACTIVITY	RESP. PARTIES	STATUS	DELIVERABLES
District Office			
1. ASCI coordinates with principals on progress toward schoolwide enrich. plan goals on regular basis	ASCI, Principal(s)	In-process	Schoolwide enrichment plan
2. Staff development presents menu of courses on differentiated curriculum, instruction, assessment for ES, teachers	DPD	Completed	Menu of courses, attendance

Abbreviations: AIS (Academic Intervention Service), **ASCI** (Assistant Superintendent for Curriculum and Instruction), **BOE** (Board of Education), **CAC** (Community Advisory Committee), **CCC** (Computer Curriculum Corp.), **CMS** (Curriculum Management System), **CPE** (Community Partnerships for Enrichment), **DCR** (Director of Community Relations), **DDM** (Director of Data Management), **DPD** (Director of Professional Development), **DPS** (Director of Pupil Services), **ES** (Enrichment Specialist), **GATES** (Gifted and Talented Education Supporters), **GS** (Grading System), **PPC** (Professional Practices Committee), **P/T** (Parent/Teacher), **RC** (Report Card), **RFP** (Request for Proposal), **Super.** (Superintendent), **UVA** (University of Virginia)

117

	KEY ACTIVITY	RESP. PARTIES	STATUS	DELIVERABLES
3.	ES attend biweekly staff development	Enrichment Team	Recurring	Agenda
4.	Offer districtwide workshops on differentiation	DPD	Recurring	Workshop programs
5.	Plan, conduct inservice for principals	ASCI	Recurring	3 day programs on focused inservice
6.	Complete K-12 study, pilot on GS & RC redesign	ASCI, ES, Principal(s)	In Process	Opportunities & recommendations
7.	Adopt K-12 GS & RC redesign	Cabinets	Not Started	Plan approved
8.	Acquire RC software, support & plan installation	Office of Super.	Not Started	Process & plan
9.	Launch & install GS/RC software, train users for phased startup	DPD	Not Started	Program & progress reports
10.	Articulate districtwide designs & processes for school-based instructional restructuring	ASCI/Principal(s)/Consultant	Not Started	Consensus guidelines
11.	Develop SEM program evaluation methods & tools	DDM	In Process	Protocols documented
12.	Benchmark, acquire & tailor new core curriculum for new 6, 7, and 8 courses (Foreign Language, Technology, Science)	ASCI	Not Started	Curriculum documents
13.	Train teachers in new curriculum for their use (Foreign Language, Technology Science)	DPD	In Process	Training schedule for each
14.	Complete plan for launch & use of new rubrics for each new core curriculum	DPD	Not Started	Plan approved
15.	Provide parent orientations to program use of CCC technology	Teachers, DPD	Not Started	Orientations @ curriculum nights, P/T meetings
16.	Develop curriculum guides (@ grade level) for parents, CAC, community groups, & CMS	ASCI	Not Started	Rough draft brochures
17.	Review & finalize Curriculum Guides with Cabinets	ASCI	Not Started	Approval
18.	Complete Curriculum Guides production & distribution	DCR	Not Started	Guides in June report cards

Abbreviations: AIS (Academic Intervention Service), **ASCI** (Assistant Superintendent for Curriculum and Instruction), **BOE** (Board of Education), **CAC** (Community Advisory Committee), **CCC** (Computer Curriculum Corp.), **CMS** (Curriculum Management System), **CPE** (Community Partnerships for Enrichment), **DCR** (Director of Community Relations), **DDM** (Director of Data Management), **DPD** (Director of Professional Development), **DPS** (Director of Pupil Services), **ES** (Enrichment Specialist), **GATES** (Gifted and Talented Education Supporters), **GS** (Grading System), **PPC** (Professional Practices Committee), **P/T** (Parent/Teacher), **RC** (Report Card), **RFP** (Request for Proposal), **Super.** (Superintendent), **UVA** (University of Virginia)

KEY ACTIVITY	RESP. PARTIES	STATUS	DELIVERABLES
19. Develop performance assessment protocol for classroom & schoolwide integration of enrichment practices	DDM	Not Started	Protocol-rubric
20. Testing K-12 implemented	AIS leader	In Process	Tests administered, results, results analyzed
21. Conduct mid-year needs assessment to identify program enhancement opportunities & supports	ASCI/ES/Principals	Not Started	Assessment analysis
22. Identify new/improved community connection models	ASCI/CAC	Not Started	List for schools, parents
23. Purchase technology to complete original program plan (including 5 computers, 1 printer, 1 TV per classroom)	ASCI/Super.	Not Started	Technology acquired & installed
24. Create & disseminate glossary of "differentiation" terms	ES Team	In Process	Glossary of terms
25. Assemble compendium of SEM newsletter articles	ASCI	In Process	Compendium
26. Develop process of ongoing dissemination of SEM news	ASCI	In Process	Flowchart
27. Coordinate & schedule enrichment specialist summer institute	ASCI/ DPD	In Process	Plan, budget and participate @ UVA
28. Update Communications Plan and continue roll-out	DCR	Recurring	Communication plan
29. Update BOE on program progress	ASCI/CAC	Recurring	BOE agenda
30. Budget, plan recruiting & initiate hiring of additional ES for middle school #2	ASCI/Principal(s)	In Process	Process, guides
Schools			
1. Enrichment specialists develop own plans to support school plan	ES	Completed	Approval by principal
2. Teachers attend workshops, staff development opportunities	Teachers	Recurring	Ongoing attendance
3. Teachers develop initial plan for classroom use of differentiation	Teachers	Completed	Approval of plans by principal
4. Teachers implement differentiation strategies in classroom	Teachers	Ongoing	Lessons, management

Abbreviations: AIS (Academic Intervention Service), **ASCI** (Assistant Superintendent for Curriculum and Instruction), **BOE** (Board of Education), **CAC** (Community Advisory Committee), **CCC** (Computer Curriculum Corp.), **CMS** (Curriculum Management System), **CPE** (Community Partnerships for Enrichment), **DCR** (Director of Community Relations), **DDM** (Director of Data Management), **DPD** (Director of Professional Development), **DPS** (Director of Pupil Services), **ES** (Enrichment Specialist), **GATES** (Gifted and Talented Education Supporters), **GS** (Grading System), **PPC** (Professional Practices Committee), **P/T** (Parent/Teacher), **RC** (Report Card), **RFP** (Request for Proposal), **Super.** (Superintendent), **UVA** (University of Virginia)

KEY ACTIVITY	RESP. PARTIES	STATUS	DELIVERABLES
5. Enrichment specialist demonstrates differentiation strategies	ES	Ongoing	Schedule
6. Teachers implement new GS & RC	Teachers	Not Started	Report cards
7. Teachers, enrichment specialist meet with principal on progress of plan	Principal	Ongoing	Implementation plan reviews
8. Observations reflect differentiation	Principal	Ongoing	Observations
9. Evaluations reflect differentiation	Principal	Not Started	Evaluations
10. Renewed staff development opportunities offered at sites	Principal	Recurring	Menu, agenda
11. Schools study internal structuring for continuity of program	Principal/CAC	Not Started	Configuration plans
12. Internal structuring improvement for program continuity planned and reported for each site	Principal	Not Started	Newsletters, brochures, etc.
13. Site Teams apply for additional resources, as school meets performance assessment protocol on differentiation	Building Enrichment Teams	Not Started	Application process, awards, recognition
14. Enrichment Specialists issue monthly SEM articles in related school specific newsletters	ES	Recurring	Forms
15. Site specific summer projects on differentiation approved, workshop days	Enrichment Specialist, Teachers, PPC	Not Started	Approval forms, differentiation

Stage II: Implementation—Phase II: Expanded Program
(Introduction of Mentoring and Enrichment Clusters, etc.)

Infrastructure			
1. Define & finalize core components of enrichment clusters and mentoring; guidelines	Cabinets	Not Started	District standards, expectations
2. Define mentoring program goals, objectives & next steps	Cabinets	Not Started	Standards, expectations, recommendations

Abbreviations: AIS (Academic Intervention Service), **ASCI** (Assistant Superintendent for Curriculum and Instruction), **BOE** (Board of Education), **CAC** (Community Advisory Committee), **CCC** (Computer Curriculum Corp.), **CMS** (Curriculum Management System), **CPE** (Community Partnerships for Enrichment), **DCR** (Director of Community Relations), **DDM** (Director of Data Management), **DPD** (Director of Professional Development), **DPS** (Director of Pupil Services), **ES** (Enrichment Specialist), **GATES** (Gifted and Talented Education Supporters), **GS** (Grading System), **PPC** (Professional Practices Committee), **P/T** (Parent/Teacher), **RC** (Report Card), **RFP** (Request for Proposal), **Super.** (Superintendent), **UVA** (University of Virginia)

KEY ACTIVITY		RESP. PARTIES	STATUS	DELIVERABLES
3.	Identify and benchmark mentoring best practice programs	Cabinets/CAC	Not Started	Findings, next steps report
4.	Finalize mentoring program direction, roles & plan	Cabinets	Not Started	Approvals
5.	Develop budget for enrichment clusters (stipends, incentives, bus costs, fees, charges, etc.)	Cabinets	In Process	Budget
6.	Establish equitable extracurricular program; in-/out-of-school (budgets, guidelines)	ES	In Process	Brochure of offerings
7.	Define options (internal & external) to address socio-emotional needs and plan next steps	Cabinets/CAC	In Process	Report
8.	Develop requirements & budget to support emotional health needs of students per building	Cabinets/CAC	In Process	Additional staff, budget, hiring
Schoolwide Enrichment Plans				
1.	Complete annual update & extension of Schoolwide Enrichment Operating Plan	Principals	Not Started	Expanded Plan
2.	Evaluate school-based models; expand knowledge of students, talents, effectiveness	Cabinets	Not Started	Literature, study, analysis, findings
3.	Initiate school-based planning for enrichment clusters	Principals	Not Started	Planning, organization process
4.	Finalize enrichment clustering plans, roles & schedules	Cabinets	Not Started	Program expectations and details
5.	Purchase materials for enrichment clusters, mentoring & extracurriculars	Teachers	Not Started	Purchase orders
6.	Recruit volunteers working with school liaisons	ES/Teachers	Not Started	Lists
7.	Coordinate leadership, transportation for before-after school extracurricular events	ES	Not Started	Menu of events
8.	Train volunteers for enrichment clusters, mentoring	ES/Teachers	Not Started	Schedules

Abbreviations: AIS (Academic Intervention Service), **ASCI** (Assistant Superintendent for Curriculum and Instruction), **BOE** (Board of Education), **CAC** (Community Advisory Committee), **CCC** (Computer Curriculum Corp.), **CMS** (Curriculum Management System), **CPE** (Community Partnerships for Enrichment), **DCR** (Director of Community Relations), **DDM** (Director of Data Management), **DPD** (Director of Professional Development), **DPS** (Director of Pupil Services), **ES** (Enrichment Specialist), **GATES** (Gifted and Talented Education Supporters), **GS** (Grading System), **PPC** (Professional Practices Committee), **P/T** (Parent/Teacher), **RC** (Report Card), **RFP** (Request for Proposal), **Super.** (Superintendent), **UVA** (University of Virginia)

121

KEY ACTIVITY	RESP. PARTIES	STATUS	DELIVERABLES
9. Launch enrichment cluster roll-out	ES	Not Started	Activity menu, schedule, process
10. Initiate mentoring program implementation	ES	Not Started	Activities and schedule
11. Coordinate, launch extra-curricular activities, transportation, communication	ES	In Process	List of procedures
12. Enroll in competitions, community service opportunities & activities, etc.	ES	Not Started	Registrations
Staff Development			
1. Plan & schedule Confratute on development & introduction of enrichment clusters	ASCI/DPD	In Process	Knowledge acquisition for application
2. Organize & conduct enrichment cluster training for principals, ES	ASCI	Not Started	Workshops
3. Expand district menu of opportunities to include Type I, II, III activities	DPD	Not Started	Menu
4. Coordinate Webster principals, ES to present SEM at national conferences	DPD	Not Started	RFP
Instruction			
1. Identify technology needs to support enhanced program(s)/activities; develop budget	Principals/ASI?:	Not Started	Tech requirements proposals & budget
2. Acquire & install additional technology required to support expanded programs, opportunities & service needs	ASCI, Super.	Not Started	Technology installed
Assessment/Evaluation			
1. Monitor & periodically report participation experience & results in competitions, enrichment clusters, mentoring	Team	Not Started	Data collection
2. Complete annual school-based SEM program self-assessment	Teachers/ES	Not Started	Forms completed

Abbreviations: AIS (Academic Intervention Service), **ASCI** (Assistant Superintendent for Curriculum and Instruction), **BOE** (Board of Education), **CAC** (Community Advisory Committee), **CCC** (Computer Curriculum Corp.), **CMS** (Curriculum Management System), **CPE** (Community Partnerships for Enrichment), **DCR** (Director of Community Relations), **DDM** (Director of Data Management), **DPD** (Director of Professional Development), **DPS** (Director of Pupil Services), **ES** (Enrichment Specialist), **GATES** (Gifted and Talented Education Supporters), **GS** (Grading System), **PPC** (Professional Practices Committee), **P/T** (Parent/Teacher), **RC** (Report Card), **RFP** (Request for Proposal), **Super.** (Superintendent), **UVA** (University of Virginia)

KEY ACTIVITY	RESP. PARTIES	STATUS	DELIVERABLES
Community Base			
1. CAC develops & maintains community resource database for each school's enrichment clustering & mentoring programs, emotional health resources & other innovations & options	CAC	Ongoing	Resource guide for schools
2. Identify and expand community partnerships for enrichment opportunities (CPE)	ASCI/CAC	Not Started	Protocols, relationships
Communication			
1. Update & expand communication plan & roll-out	Community Relations	In Process	Plan
2. Develop & implement a districtwide & school-based recognition program for exemplary efforts & results for students, teachers & volunteers/mentors, etc.	ASCI/Cabinets/CAC	Not Started	Recognition design, process
3. Establish showcases (& exhibits) of exemplary work	Teachers	Ongoing	Publicity

Abbreviations: AIS (Academic Intervention Service), **ASCI** (Assistant Superintendent for Curriculum and Instruction), **BOE** (Board of Education), **CAC** (Community Advisory Committee), **CCC** (Computer Curriculum Corp.), **CMS** (Curriculum Management System), **CPE** (Community Partnerships for Enrichment), **DCR** (Director of Community Relations), **DDM** (Director of Data Management), **DPD** (Director of Professional Development), **DPS** (Director of Pupil Services), **ES** (Enrichment Specialist), **GATES** (Gifted and Talented Education Supporters), **GS** (Grading System), **PPC** (Professional Practices Committee), **P/T** (Parent/Teacher), **RC** (Report Card), **RFP** (Request for Proposal), **Super.** (Superintendent), **UVA** (University of Virginia)

JOB ANNOUNCEMENT FOR SEM PROGRAM FACILITATOR

Gaston County School District Vacancy Announcement*

Position: Schoolwide Enrichment Model Program Facilitator

Qualifications:

1. A thorough knowledge of the components of the Schoolwide Enrichment Model.
2. A North Carolina Gifted Education Licensure or university credits equal to the state requirement for licensure.
3. Master's degree from an accredited university or in progress.
4. Knowledge and experience with the following:
    *   Curriculum modification techniques such as curriculum compacting
    *   Multiple Intelligences
    *   Cluster Grouping
    *   Enrichment Clusters
    *   Interest Inventories
    *   Learning Style Profiles
    *   Project-Based Learning
    *   Differentiation
    *   Research-based best teaching practices
5. Exceptional communication skills.
6. Effective leadership skills that effectively exhibit team problem-solving.
7. Effective interpersonal skills with diverse groups of students, administrators, colleagues, and parents.
8. Experience presenting professional development.
9. Strong demonstration of computer skills and experience with utilizing technology integration and product/performance assessments.

Responsibilities:

1. Leadership in program development, staff development, and the infusion of enrichment know-how and materials into the school.
    *   Lead the school staff in developing and implementing an organizational plan for delivering enrichment and acceleration through an integrated continuum of services: The Schoolwide Enrichment Model
    *   Create a Schoolwide Enrichment Model Team and serve as the chair.
    *   Consult with administrators at the school site to implement the components of the Schoolwide Enrichment Model that will serve as a blueprint for total school improvement.

*Developed by Gaston County Schools, Gastonia, NC. Used with permission.

- Assist the school in identifying and developing talents of young people by systemically assessing their strengths providing enrichment opportunities, resources, and services.
- Facilitate the organization of enrichment clusters by leading the SEM team in the development of a schedule, recruiting volunteer facilitators, placing students, and providing an opportunity to share and celebrate products.
- Facilitate the planning/scheduling of visiting speakers, field trips, artistic performances, and other grade level, schoolwide, and interest group activities that are designed to expand the scope of the overall school experience.
- Help establish learning communities that honor ethnic, gender, and cultural diversity and promote mutual respect.
- Foster the implementation of a collaborative school culture that includes appropriate decision-making opportunities for students, parents, teachers, and administrators.
- Review a wide array of enrichment materials and determine where within the regular curriculum these materials might be most effectively used in the classroom to help improve the academic performance of all students.
- Involve parents in planning home-based enrichment activities, tutoring, and the completion of challenging homework assignments.
- Attending local, state, and national conferences to enhance leadership skills pertinent to position.

2. Act as a resource consultant, peer coach, and facilitator to the teacher's role and student's role in Schoolwide Enrichment Model.

- Assist teachers in using a flexible approach to curricular differentiation (such as curriculum compacting) and the optimal use of learning time.
- Consult with school staff to develop differentiated, open-ended, or product-oriented assignments to address individual differences.
- Encourage the use of a variety of small/large group teaching strategies to ensure student engagement and optimal learning.
- Coach teachers in developing and using problem-solving simulations and activities that require creativity and the use of higher level thinking skills.
- Provide students with resources, coaching, and supervision of projects that are extensions of the regular classroom, enrichment clusters, or high interests.

PROGRAM PROGRESS REPORT FOR PARENTS
Schoolwide Enrichment Model in Our School District*

What has been accomplished so far with the new Schoolwide Enrichment Model in Webster?
To date, the district has hired eight enrichment specialists. All are certified, experienced teachers who also attended the University of Connecticut for a week's training in the Schoolwide Enrichment Model. Each of the elementary and middle schools has organized an Enrichment Team who, with the full faculty, has developed a Schoolwide Enrichment Plan. Teachers have identified enrichment strategies that they will develop and refine in a variety of subject areas. Teachers and principals continue to attend and present workshops to their colleagues about increasing knowledge about curriculum differentiation strategies, student ability and interests, student self-systems, and complex reasoning processes.

Monthly articles are written for parents in the school newsletters, brochures were sent home in September, a video describing SEM was shown on Channel 15 in the fall, and an SEM web site linked to the school district's web site. Four presentations to the Board of Education have been televised to inform the community about SEM progress.

Tell me about the Schoolwide Enrichment Model at my child's school.
Every elementary and middle school developed a Schoolwide Enrichment Plan that focuses on increasing teachers' capacity to deliver differentiated strategies in the classroom, providing challenge to the students. Teachers are refining activities, tests, materials and assignments so students are challenged and continue to learn. Schools are working on curriculum compacting in math and spelling, literature circles, tiered assignments, cubing, complex reasoning, habits of mind, and student self-systems to name a few. While there is a benefit for all, there is a special focus on providing challenging activities and materials for our very able learners. Call your school principal if you would like more information about the Schoolwide Enrichment Plan from your school.

How does my child participate in SEM?
Every child participates because the model is designed for differentiating activities in every classroom. The goal is to keep children challenged and interested in learning, developing his or her talents. It may show up in any or all subjects. For many children, instruction directed to grade level expectations is exactly right. Some children need more difficult reading levels, opportunities to express themselves verbally or physically rather than in writing, choices in the kinds of projects they will produce, easier or more difficult math or spelling assignments. It also focuses upon an entire class participating in an activity that is rich in complex reasoning, with everyone thinking deeply about new knowledge. These are all ways that a teacher differentiates instruction, and it provides challenge and interest. If you have questions or concerns about your child's assignments, do not hesitate to call the classroom teacher or the enrichment specialist.

*Developed by Ellen Agostinelli, Webster Central School District, Webster, NY. Used with permission.

What are the next steps?

- A questionnaire will be sent home for parents this spring asking for your input about the Schoolwide Enrichment Model. Teachers, principals, enrichment specialists also will be surveyed and a compilation of results will be available over the summer.

- Staff development will continue over the summer and throughout the school year.

- We expect to hire a ninth enrichment specialist, giving every elementary and middle school its own staff member.

- Teachers will continue to focus on developing and refining differentiation strategies to challenge each student.

- Schools will continue to concentrate efforts on Complex Reasoning Processes that teach children to think deeply about new knowledge.

- Schools will be preparing to offer Enrichment Clusters during the next year, coordinating small, multi-grade groups that investigate issues of interest.

- Look for the new software on classroom computers that will enable students to progress in reading, writing, and math at their own rates.

- The district will be assessing resources in the schools that address student social and emotional development and forwarding recommendations for alternative approaches and budget implications.

- A resource book of community members interested in volunteering as enrichment cluster leaders and mentors in the schools will be developed.

- A new report card is under review that will reflect student efforts and achievements, including enrichment areas. We anticipate a final product by the end of next year.

How can I learn more about enrichment opportunities at my school?

Every month the school newsletter includes an article about enrichment at your school. Articles describe classroom activities, list upcoming events, and explain enrichment vocabulary used at school. If your child is not showing you the school's newsletter each month, check the backpack!

Each school developed a Schoolwide Enrichment Plan with its Enrichment Team and full faculty. It outlines the school's enrichment goals, workshops and activities for the year. Your classroom teacher, your principal, and your school's enrichment specialist always welcome your questions and are a great resource to you.

What more can I do?

The goal here is to develop your child's talents. Have you contacted the museum or art gallery for classes? Have you enriched your vacation plans with side trips to historical places, galleries, work studios and architectural landmarks? Have you inquired with the scouts about starting a book club? Does your child have enough time every day for unstructured creative play, whether outside, in the attic, or with friends? Have you encouraged friendships by inviting other children to your home? Do you model for your child a curious attitude about life, asking "I wonder" questions, trying new things, admitting a mistake, working hard and persevering at difficult projects, thinking out loud as you work out a solution to a problem, spending time with each child to get to know his or her interests, abilities and talents? If you need more ideas, feel welcome to talk with your child's teacher and the enrichment specialist.

For more information, check the district web site at www.websterschools.org or contact your child's teacher or the enrichment specialist at your school.

GRANT PROPOSAL TO FUND SEM ACTIVITIES

Developing Talents in all Students at Southeast School*

[1] One Paragraph Summary

This grant proposal will enable the administration, faculty, parents and students at Southeast School in Mansfield, Connecticut to implement the Schoolwide Enrichment Model (SEM), a plan for developing talent in all students. The SEM was originally created as a programming model for gifted students. Recently, however, the developer of the model, Dr. Joseph Renzulli, has written a book entitled Schools for Talent Development in which he advocates the use of this model as a method for school improvement. A few schools in the country have implemented this approach, and we hope to be the first in Connecticut to adapt this model. The SEM has three major goals: (1) developing talents in all children; (2) providing a broad range of advanced-level enrichment experiences for all students; and (3) using the ways that students respond to these enrichment experiences as stepping stones for follow-up learning. The SEM has three components: (1) The Total Talent Portfolio (individual portfolios for talent development in each child focusing on abilities, interests and learning styles). (See Appendix A) (2.) Curriculum modification including a system entitled Curriculum Compacting (a method for substituting work students may already know for enrichment and acceleration activities); textbook analysis and curriculum mapping; and expanding the depth of learning to enable students to learn something they select in an advanced manner and (3) enrichment teaching and learning which takes into account the uniqueness of each learner, and the enjoyment of learning experiences.

[2] Reason the proposal has been submitted

This grant describes a plan that has demonstrated its effectiveness in bringing about significant changes in schooling. The plan, entitled the Schoolwide Enrichment Model (SEM), was originally developed as a program model in gifted education and includes a systematic set of specific strategies for increasing student effort, enjoyment, and performance, and for integrating a broad range of advanced level learning experiences and higher order thinking skills. The general approach of the SEM is one of infusing more effective practices into existing school structures rather than layering on additional things for schools to do. This research supported plan is designed for general education, but it is based on a large number of instructional methods and curricular practices that had their origins in special programs for high ability students. Special programs of almost any type have been the true laboratories of our nation's schools because they have presented ideal opportunities for testing new ideas and experimenting with potential solutions to long-standing educational problems. Programs for high potential students have been an especially fertile place for experimentation because such programs usually are not encumbered by prescribed curriculum guides or tra-

---

* Grant written by the planning committee at Southeast School in Mansfield, Connecticut. Reproduced with permission.

ditional methods of instruction. It was within the context of these programs that the thinking skills movement first took hold in American education, and the pioneering work of notable theorists such as Benjamin Bloom, Howard Gardner, and Robert Sternberg first gained the attention of the education community. Other developments that had their origins in special programs are currently being examined for general practice. These developments include: a focus on concept rather than skill learning, the use of interdisciplinary curriculum and theme-based studies, student portfolios, performance assessment, cross-grade grouping, alternative scheduling patterns, and perhaps most important, opportunities for students to exchange traditional roles as lesson-learners and doers-of-exercises for more challenging and demanding roles that require hands-on learning, first-hand investigations, and the application of knowledge and thinking skills to complex problems.

Research opportunities in a variety of special programs allowed us to develop instructional procedures and programming alternatives that emphasize the need (1) to provide a broad range of advanced level enrichment experiences for all students, and (2) to use the many and varied ways that students respond to these experiences as stepping stones for relevant follow-up on the parts of individuals or small groups. This approach is not viewed as a new way to identify who is or is not "gifted!" Rather, the process simply identifies how subsequent opportunities, resources, and encouragement can be provided to support continuous escalations of student involvement in both required and self-selected activities. This approach to the development of high levels of multiple potentials in young people is purposefully designed to sidestep the traditional practice of labeling some students "gifted" and instead, places giftedness in a developmental perspective. Thus, for example, we speak and write about the development of gifted behaviors in specific areas of learning and human expression. This orientation has allowed many students opportunities to develop high levels of creative and productive accomplishments that otherwise would have been denied through traditional special program models.

Practices that have been a mainstay of many special programs for "the gifted" are being absorbed into general education by reform models designed to upgrade the performance of all students. This integration of gifted program know-how is viewed as a favorable development for two reasons. First, the adoption of many special program practices is indicative of the viability and usefulness of both the know-how of special programs and the role enrichment specialists can and should play in total school improvement. Second, all students should have opportunities to develop higher order thinking skills and to pursue more rigorous content and first-hand investigative activities than those typically found in today's "dumbed down" textbooks. The ways in which students respond to enriched learning experiences should be used as a rationale for providing all students with advanced level follow-up opportunities. This approach reflects a democratic ideal that accommodates the full range of individual differences in the entire student population, and it opens the door to programming models that develop the talent potentials of many at-risk students who traditionally have been excluded from anything but the most basic types of curricular experiences. The application of gifted program know-how into general education is supported by a wide variety of research on human abilities (Bloom, 1985; Gardner, 1983; Renzulli, 1986; Sternberg, 1984). Indeed, Hank Levin, the developer of the Accelerated Schools Project, urges general education to use gifted education strategies for all students. This research clearly and unequivocally provides a justification for much broader conceptions of talent development.

Although everyone has a stake in good schools, America has been faced with a school problem: that has resulted in declining confidence in schools and the people who work in them, drastic limitations in the amount of financial support for education, and general public apathy or dissatisfaction with the quality of education our young people are receiving. The parents of poor children have given up hope that education will enable their sons and daughters to break the bonds of poverty. And the middle class, perhaps for the first time in our nation's history, is exploring government supported alternatives such as vouchers and tax credits for private schools, home schooling, charter schools, and summer and after-school programs that enhance admission to competitive colleges. In this grant, we hope to more fully implement a program that focuses on talent development in all children, which we believe represents a fundamental rethinking of how schools are run.

The instructional procedures and programming alternatives that characterize the Schoolwide Enrichment Model have three goals:

1. Develop the talents of all of our students
2. Provide a broad range of advanced-level enrichment experiences for all students.
3. Use the many and varied ways that students respond to these experiences as stepping stones for relevant follow-up.

The model has its roots in special programs for high-potential students. Such programs have proved an especially fertile place for experimentation, because they're usually not encumbered by prescribed curriculum guides or by traditional methods of instruction. Many school improvement concepts that originated in special programs have begun to surface in general education. These include, for example, a focus on concept rather than skill learning, an interdisciplinary curriculum and theme-based studies, student portfolios, cross-grade grouping, and alternative scheduling patterns.

In addition, the enrichment approach reflects the democratic ideal that schools can accommodate the full range of individual differences. Traditional identification procedures restrict services to small numbers of high-scoring students. Enrichment activities, however, enable schools to help develop the talents of all students who manifest their potentials in many other ways.

Essential Elements

Bringing the Schoolwide Enrichment Model to large segments of the school population requires three components:

1. The Total Talent Portfolio. The model focuses on specific learning characteristics that can serve as a basis for talent development. The approach uses both traditional and performance-based assessment to determine three dimensions of the learner—abilities, interests, and preferred learning styles. This information, which focuses on strengths rather than deficits, is compiled into a form called the Total Talent Portfolio. Schools use the portfolios to decide which talent development opportunities to offer a particular student through regular classes, enrichment clusters, and special services.

2.   Curriculum modification techniques. The Schoolwide Enrichment Model relies upon a curriculum that challenges all students to learn, offers a number of in-depth learning experiences, and injects enrichment opportunities into the school's regular activities. Modifying the curriculum typically involves the following procedures:

- Curriculum compacting. Through this process, schools eliminate repetition of previously mastered material, upgrade the challenge level of the regular curriculum, and provide time for enrichment and acceleration activities (Reis & Renzulli, 1992). In many ways, curriculum compacting is simply common sense—it imitates the pattern that teachers naturally follow when individualizing instruction or teaching without textbooks.

- Textbook analysis. The textbook is the curriculum in the overwhelming majority of to-day's classrooms. Despite much rhetoric about school and curriculum reform, that situation isn't likely to change soon. As a result, modifying the curriculum will necessarily involve an in-depth analysis of current textbooks.

- Expanding the depth of learning. This third procedure for modifying curriculum is based on the work of Phenix (1964), who found that focusing on representative concepts and ideas is the best way to capture the essence of a topic. Representative ideas—themes, patterns, main features, sequences, and organizing structures—often serve as the basis for interdisciplinary or multidisciplinary studies.

Beyond those concepts, in-depth learning requires increasingly complex information that moves up the hierarchy of knowledge: for example, from facts to trends and sequences, to classifications and categories, to principles and generalizations, and then to theories and structures. The dimension of learning commonly referred to as process or thinking skills is another form of content. These skills form the cognitive structures and problem-solving strategies that endure long after students have forgotten the facts or trends.

Lastly, in-depth learning involves the application of methods to problems. In other words, the student takes on the role of firsthand investigator rather than the more passive learner of lessons.

3.   Enrichment Learning and Teaching. The third component needed to put the Schoolwide Enrichment Model into practice is based on the ideas of philosophers and researchers ranging from William James and John Dewey to Howard Gardner and Albert Bandura. The work of this small but influential group, coupled with our own research, has given rise to the concept of enrichment learning and teaching. Four principles define this concept:

- Each learner is unique.
- Learning is more effective when students enjoy what they're doing.
- Learning is more meaningful and enjoyable when content (for example, knowledge) and process (for example, thinking skills) have a real problem as their context.
- Enrichment learning and teaching focus on enhancing knowledge and acquiring thinking skills.

As outlined later, we have had an effort to plan for the implementation of this model for the past two years. Through participation in meetings with our parents group (PTO) and faculty and staff we developed an Enrichment Team that has implemented a number of enrichment opportunities for all students. For example, we have implemented an enrichment cluster component (we were the first school in Connecticut to implement this program which is now being replicated in 10 or 12 other schools in the state). We have initiated a number of other enrichment opportunities for all students such as assembly programs, after-school programs, Science Fairs, Family Math events. Our preliminary planning has resulted in a diverse offering of numerous enrichment opportunities. However, in order to move to the next level of implementation in which we develop Talent Portfolios for all students, implement curriculum modification techniques and more fully implement enrichment learning and teaching, we need to have our enrichment specialist on a full-time basis as she is currently scheduled for half-time at our school. We also need to be able to provide our classroom teachers with staff development in teaching thinking skills (enrichment teaching and learning) in curriculum modification and in the other components of the model.

*See the enclosed article from *Educational Leadership* that mentions our cluster programs [not included in *The Administrator's Guide to the Schoolwide Enrichment Model*].

[3] How the project fits with other change efforts

In the last two years, we have made significant efforts to institute three change efforts. We have instituted curriculum mapping with a focus on interdisciplinary instruction. We have also implemented a block scheduling procedure which facilitates to enable uninterrupted blocks of time and less fragmentation of instructional time, as well as fewer pullouts. We are also involved in the early intervention program which enhances classroom modification for all children with special needs. The implementation of the SEM fits well within our overall district goals and our previous efforts at change. Our superintendent has written a position paper on curriculum modification, curriculum differentiation, and enrichment. The district has adopted the Effective Schools Model. A publication entitled "High Expectations for All" was written by a committee of teachers, administrators, and interested others that is included in Appendix.Our district mission statement which is included in this publication stresses that the curriculum must remain flexible and be tailored to suit the needs of individual students. The two other elementary schools in our district have begun enrichment clusters, following our lead.

We believe that schools are being bombarded with proposals for change, which range from total systemic reform to tinkering with bits and pieces of subjects and teaching methods. Often the proposals seem little more than lists of intended goals or outcomes, with limited direction provided. Effective and lasting change occurs only when it's initiated, nurtured, and monitored from within the school itself. External regulations and remedies seldom change the daily behaviors of students and teachers. Nor do they deal effectively with solutions to internal school problems (Barth 1990).

The change process recommended in the Schoolwide Enrichment Model begins with an examination of the major factors affecting the quality of learning in a school. These factors, may be internal (within the school) or external, but all inter-relate. For example, an internal building principal may be externally influenced if central administration makes staffing assignments; state regulations or districtwide textbook policies may externally influence the internal curriculum. The Schoolwide Enrichment Model doesn't replace existing structures but rather seeks to improve them by concentrating on the factors that have a direct bearing on learning.

[4] Persons involved in developing the proposal

The principal, teachers, and representatives of parent groups and the central office formed a planning committee. There are only three guidelines for the planning committee as it embarks on a process for exploring the plan presented in this proposal. (The word exploring is emphasized because consensus was reached at each step of the process in order for the plan to work.) First, all planning committee members were provided with information about the Schoolwide Enrichment Model so that they were well informed and engaged in discussions and debate about whether or not they are interested in the plan. All planning committee members had equal rights and opportunities to express their opinions. A majority decision was reached to recommend the plan to the school community at large, and information was made available to all faculty and parents.

The planning committee arranged a series of discussion group meetings that were open to and included members of all groups within the school. groups. Printed information, key diagrams and charts, and the results of planning committee deliberations was brought to the attention of the discussion groups. The meetings continued until everyone had a chance to express his or her opinions, after which a vote was taken as to whether or not to proceed with the plan. Results from each discussion group were reported to the planning committee. The planning committee met with the assistant superintendent and appropriate central office personnel. Once again, descriptive material about the model was provided, and the model characterized as a pilot or experimental venture. Assurances should be given that there is no intention to replace any of the programs or initiatives that the district has already adopted. Our goal was to infuse exemplary learning and teaching opportunities into the existing school frameworks. During the 1994-95 school year, we initiated a series of enrichment clusters in the fall and spring semester and provided training for teachers in various aspects of enrichment teaching and learning.

[5] How the project will improve student achievement and how it represents a fundamental rethinking of how teaching and learning are organized

Since this model attempts to develop talents in all students through the use of the total talent portfolio, enrichment teaching and learning and curriculum modification, our goals encompass increasing achievement and motivation in all students. We believe that motivation is increased when students enjoy learning, and when they are able to select certain components of their learning as discussed in section two above:

Implementation of the SEM begins by placing the act of learning at the center of the change process. Organizational and administrative structures such as vouchers, site based management, school choice, multi-aged classes, parent involvement, and extended school days are important considerations, but they do not address directly the crucial question of how we can improve what happens in classrooms where teachers, students, and curriculum interact with one another. In the SEM, all recommendations for school improvement are based on the learning process. A figural representation of the learning process used in the SEM is depicted in Figure 1. The "Learner Circle" highlights important components that students bring to the act of learning. Thus we must take into consideration: (1) present achievement levels of students in each area of study, (2) the learner's interest in particular topics and the ways in which we can enhance present interests or develop new interests, and (3) the preferred styles of learning that will improve the learner's motivation to pursue the material that is being studied. Likewise, the teacher and learner dimensions have subcomponents that must be considered when we place the act of learning at the center of the school improvement process (Renzulli, 1992).

[6] The Change Process

As mentioned earlier, the change process involves a number of groups and a number of steps. We developed a planning committee consisting of the Principal, the Assistant Superintendent for Curriculum and Instruction, the Enrichment Specialist, two representative classroom teachers, two PTO members and two professors from the School of Education at The University of Connecticut.

[7] Budget Summary and Narrative

Personnel: An amount of $17,500 is budgeted in order to enable us to extend the half-time enrichment teacher currently allocated to our school to a full time position to enable us to be able to implement the various components explained in this grant. Ms. Susan Lindsay will increase her position from half to full-time.

Evaluator: An outside evaluator will complete a comprehensive evaluation on the program as described in the proposal. Dr. Sally Reis has agreed to provide this evaluation contract as an inkind contribution for $5,000.

Consultant: Dr. Joseph Renzulli of the School of Education at The University of Connecticut has agreed to provide consultant services which are also an inkind contribution of approximately $10, 000.00.

Materials and Supplies: A computer (Power Mac and Style) will enable us to network with various enrichment opportunities and to be able to complete desk top publishing for student products.

An inkind contribution of approximately $1300.00 will be made for supplies such as software, America on Line Subscription Fees, and other supplies necessary for implementation.

Meeting and Convening: An amount is requested for various staff development sessions including training in curriculum modification, enrichment teaching and learning and the use of the total talent portfolio. In addition, we have made arrangements with the Teaching the Talented Program at the University of Connecticut to enable approximately ten of our staff members to attend strands at the Summer Institute at The University of Connecticut (See Appendix) to receive additional training in Talents Unlimited and other enrichment teaching opportunities.

Program Activities: We are requesting funds to enable us to bring certain enrichment opportunities to the school. We will use the funds to schedule certain schoolwide enrichment opportunities such as visiting artists, visiting authors, speakers and other opportunities.

Others: We are also requesting funds for printing and publication of student work such as children's' books, schoolwide newspapers, poetry books, art projects and any other work from students that is developed as a part of this grant.

[8] Stakeholders

Our primary group of stakeholders in the schools are all students who will benefit from the adoption of a policy in which we attempt to develop talents in all of our students. We also believe parents will benefit as we seek their input and their help in creating a school environment which emphasizes talent development. By providing staff development for all faculty and staff in enrichment teaching and learning, the Total Talent Portfolio and curriculum modification, we will also be addressing the needs of the faculty for on-going staff development that they have selected and been an active partner in choosing to implement. We also hope that other teachers and administrators will be potential stakeholders. Dozens of persons have visited our school to observe our enrichment clusters. We have sent out hundreds of descriptions of this first component of the SEM that we have developed. We hope to disseminate information and implementation strategies about the other components that we cannot implement unless we receive this grant.

[9] Evaluation

Dr. Sally Reis has agreed to be the external evaluator for our grant as an "inkind" contribution. Currently, Dr. Reis is an Associate Professor of Educational Psychology at The University of Connecticut. She has had extensive experience in evaluating educational programs, and is currently completing two large scale evaluations. The first is for a National Science Foundation grant to Talcott Mt. Science Center and the second is an evaluation of the elementary language arts curriculum in a large Connecticut school district.

The evaluation will employ a matrix sample design in which various components of the SEM will be evaluated by key stakeholder groups periodically throughout the academic school year. For example, parent and teacher attitudes about enrichment teaching and learning will be assessed at the beginning and at the end of the school year. Student attitudes about enrichment opportunities will be assessed as will changes in interests and content area preferences before and after their participation in enrichment clusters and various other enrichment opportunities.

The use of advanced content will also be investigated and documented in various enrichment offerings. Products completed by students will be assessed using valid and reliable student product assessment forms. Teachers will be interviewed about the use of talent portfolios and the number of talent portfolios completed for students will be documented.

Various strategies for curriculum modification will be documented and evaluations will be conducted on this specific strategies. For example, when curriculum compacting occurs, an instrument to assess the compacting process will be used to evaluate how this specific curriculum modification strategy used by Southeast School teachers compares to a national sample of teachers who have implemented compacting. this approach to evaluation will enable us to collect a wealth of information from specific groups of stakeholders who will each benefit from certain components of the model.

10. **Budget Summary and Work Plan--See attached** [not included in *Opening Doors: The Administrator's Guide to the Schoolwide Enrichment Model*].

11. **Attachments** [not included in *Opening Doors: The Administrator's Guide to the Schoolwide Enrichment Model*]

    A. The Strategic School Profile of Mansfield
    B. The district Philosophy is included in the document High Expectations for All.
    C. The school mission statement.
    D. The district's mission statement and annual goals
    E. The contract between The Mansfield Board of Education and The Mansfield Education Association.
    F. Letter from Superintendent of Schools and Appropriate Documents

APPENDIX C: PROFESSIONAL DEVELOPMENT ACTIVITIES

Activity A: Leaving a Lasting Legacy

PURPOSE:	**To discuss influences on career paths**
TIME:	**20-30 minutes**
SETTING:	**Participants at tables**
MATERIALS:	**Paper, markers, overhead projector or flip chart**
DESIGNATION:	**Essential**

This activity engages participants in sharing and self-reflection. The knowledge you gain about your staff through this activity will help you explain to your staff how SEM will support them in fulfilling what they hope to be as educators.

Divide participants into small groups and ask everyone to share with their colleagues why they became educators and who may have influenced their decision to enter the profession. Do they have the passion to pass on the legacy to others? Ask them to think back to the gifts they received from a mentor/educator and then think forward to the gifts that they can bring to a child. Though this activity may seem very simplistic, the reasons participants chose to become educators are incredibly varied, and the discussion can remind participants of the influence those who may have inspired them had. Have volunteers share their stories to the larger group and call attention to any trends.

Activity B: Professional Promenade

PURPOSE:	**To discuss what makes an excellent education**
TIME:	**20-30 minutes**
SETTING:	**Weather permitting, somewhere outside**
MATERIALS:	**Paper, markers, overhead projector or flip chart, clipboard for participants (one per group), *Fish! Sticks* video (optional)**
DESIGNATION:	**Essential**

This activity engages participants in self-reflection and discussion. Before organizing participants into small groups, initiate a discussion on what learning and teaching should be. To inspire this type of discussion, you may wish to have participants view a video entitled *Fish! Sticks*. This amusing video describes how a sleepy little fish market in Seattle became world famous when employees developed a vision. (See Appendix E for more information on this video.)

On a flip chart or overhead projector list one or two beliefs (e.g., there are many ways to be smart, there are many ways to group students for instruction, etc.). Divide participants into small groups and ask them to share with each other what they envision for students in their school: What do they believe translates into an excellent education? What should the school environment look like? Ask participants to take a clipboard and marker and, as a group, move to a spot on the school campus to discuss their beliefs. Encouraging groups to go outside moves them to a more relaxed environment where some participants may feel more comfortable sharing their thoughts. If the weather is bad, participants can either stay where they are or move to another room in the building. Ask a volunteer in each group to record the group's beliefs. Return to the meeting room and have each group recorder present his or her list to the larger group. List responses on a large chart or overhead projector titled "At [insert name of school] We Believe . . ." This discussion helps set the stage for aligning beliefs with actual practices by showing how SEM matches what they say provides an excellent education for students.

Note: You may want to turn the final list into a large poster to place on display in a heavily trafficked area of the school (e.g., a main hallway). The poster could include a "Photo Gallery" of students/staff engaged in the activities on the list. The teachers in my school believe in interest-based learning so we display photographs of students participating in enrichment clusters and Type I activities.

Activity C: Classroom Practices

PURPOSE:	**To examine whether current classroom practices are aligned with beliefs about good teaching**
TIME:	**Approximately 10 minutes**
SETTING:	**Participants take checklist home, then return for general discussion session**
MATERIALS:	**Compacting Readiness Checklist and pencil**
DESIGNATION:	**Optional**

Prior to the session, distribute the Compacting Readiness Checklist (Starko, 1986). Ask participants to complete the checklist and bring it to a discussion session scheduled within a few days of distribution. Make sure participants know that you will not collect the checklists. They are a tool to help the participants identify discrepancies between their personal beliefs about good teaching and their classroom practices. Explain how to interpret the results: If there is an approximate 1:1 ratio between Part A and Part B, then there is a good alignment between a teacher's beliefs and his or her classroom practices. If their is a discrepancy between Part A and Part B (Part A yields a much higher number than Part B), then the results are more like the many teachers who have a difficult time making their beliefs come alive in the classroom setting.

The checklist opens the door to understanding the many factors that can cause practices to diverge from beliefs (e.g., mandates, standardized testing, too many educational initiatives, etc.). At the discussion session, ask participants why they think teaching practices might differ from beliefs about what makes good teaching. Participants can speak in general terms or talk specifically about their own experience. Explain that further discussions in other activities will focus on ways that SEM helps teachers recapture the excitement and creativity they hope for in their teaching.

Note: Some administrators encourage participants to leave anonymous notes in the facilitator's mailbox during the week following distribution of the checklist. The facilitator can then address the anonymous comments in the group discussion.

Compacting Readiness Checklist*
Part A

	Yes	No

1. I believe students learn at different rates. _____ _____

2. I believe students come to me with differing amounts of knowledge. Some do not have adequate background to master the regular curriculum while others have already mastered some materials. _____ _____

3. I believe students should prove mastery of regular curriculum at my grade level. _____ _____

4. I believe that students can learn through a variety of large group, small group, and individual activities. _____ _____

5. I believe that students should be provided with work which is challenging and appropriate to their ability level. _____ _____

6. I believe students have different interests. _____ _____

7. I believe *some* of a student's work should be based on his/her interests and strengths. _____ _____

Total Yes Responses: _____

x 10

Total: _____

Part B

Please think about the activities in your classroom yesterday.

	Yes	No

1. Yesterday I assigned homework or seatwork. All students completed the same assignment. _____ _____

2. Yesterday one of my students completed his/her assignment before the rest of the class. Did I assign more work of a similar nature? _____ _____

3. Did any student receive an "A" or 100% on all work completed yesterday? _____ _____

4. Did any student complete his/her work before others and spend time in "less than productive" ways (comic books, airplanes, sleep)? _____ _____

5. Were any above-average ability students discipline or behavior problems yesterday? _____ _____

Total No Responses: _____

x 10

Total: _____

continues on next page

*Reprinted from Starko, A. J. (1986). *It's about time: Inservice strategies for curriculum compacting.* Mansfield Center, CT: Creative Learning Press.

Compacting Readiness Checklist

Part B (continued)

Bonus Questions: Add 10 points for each YES answer

	Yes	No
6. At least one student spent time yesterday working on a project in his/her interest area which was *not* part of a class assignment.	_____	_____
7. I have given a pretest in_____. At least one student was excused from exercises in materials already mastered.	_____	_____

Total Bonus Points: _____

Total for Part B: _____

What is your readiness ratio?

Total Part A: _____

Total Part B: _____

Activity D: From Paper to Reality

PURPOSE:	**Relating SEM on paper to classroom realities**
TIME:	**45-60 minutes**
SETTING:	**Small groups of six to eight arranged in a circle**
MATERIALS:	**Multiple copies of an article or excerpt from a book about SEM, highlighters, marker, index cards, pens or pencils**
DESIGNATION:	**Essential**

This activity can solidify participants' connections with each other and their understandings about SEM and its various components. Participants will discuss how the model matches what they said they believe in and value for their students. The activity can be conducted in a variety of settings, including faculty meeting, grade level meeting, etc.

Distribute a short article or book excerpt on SEM at the beginning of the session. Ask participants to silently read the text and select one statement from the article that they feel "says it all." Ask the participants to record the statement on an index card and note where the statement is (page #, paragraph #), when everyone is finished, break up into small groups. Ask for a volunteer in each group to begin by reading the statement he or she chose. Each person in the discussion group (except the reader) then responds to the statement. For example, one participant might choose the statement, "Enjoyment and interest can be the very ember to ignite a true love of learning" and another might offer the following response: "I can recall a tremendous burst of interest from a little boy in my class whenever we spoke about airplanes. He knew everything about how they worked, what they were made of, and all about their designs. I saw a spark in him that I don't typically see, and I was impressed with his wealth of knowledge. This sentence that you selected made me think of him." Participants do not have to contribute a response to each statement read. After everyone has a chance to react, the reader gets "the final word," elaborating on why he or she selected the excerpt. The process continues until everyone has read his or her statement.

Note: If time is limited you may wish to provide the article and materials prior to the session. In a memorandum, provide the directions to read the article, underline or highlight text that evokes meaning, and note where the text is. Explain that at the faculty meeting everyone will be organized into small groups to react to the text.

Activity E: Facing Challenges

PURPOSE:	To address possible challenges to implementation
TIME:	10-15 minutes
SETTING:	Participants at tables
MATERIALS:	Paper, markers, overhead projector or flip chart
DESIGNATION:	Essential

Divide participants into small groups. Ask each group to brainstorm challenges that they may face during implementation. Some typical responses are funding, time, and staff development, etc. The list below presents a sample list of challenges generated by a group of educators who participated in this activity. Generally, the lists of challenges are consistent from school to school. Don't be surprised if your teachers generate a similar list.

Challenges

- identifying link between SEM/assessments/accountability/district mandates/curriculum
- getting parents involved
- taking what teachers do and expanding upon it
- scheduling
- getting true commitment
- finding the time
- minimizing teacher reluctance/resistance
- adapting model to the school
- funding
- finding best way to approach professional development
- evaluation

Invite each group to share their top three challenges with the whole group, instructing participants to avoid repeating any challenge already shared. Record challenges on chart paper or transparency for future reference. Assure participants that as you progress through the implementation process, each challenge will be addressed and checked off the list. Within a day or two of the meeting provide each participant with the list of challenges and ask them to think about how they can overcome them. Set a tone that move s teachers from focusing on the challenges alone to "How can we do this?" Tell them to meet as a grade level and generate at least three ways to conquer some of the challenges on the list. It's best if you don't participate in this meeting. After each grade level has met (don't forget your special area teachers), arrange another faculty meeting with the agenda "Overcoming Challenges." Once again, organize teachers into discussion groups to talk about their solutions. Be sure to generate a list of their suggestions that everyone can refer to as the school moves through the implementation process. This brief activity can help reduce the anxiety teachers feel whenever a shift in teaching practices occur. It demonstrates your commitment that their voices will be heard throughout the implementation process.

Activity F: Enrichment Cluster Simulation

PURPOSE:	**To introduce enrichment clusters**
TIME:	**Approximately one hour**
SETTING:	**Large group**
MATERIALS:	**Chart paper and display easel, colored markers, tacks or masking tape, Comparison Sheet, Sample Enrichment Cluster Sheet, Cluster Simulation Worksheet (one per group), and a pencil**
DESIGNATION:	**ESSENTIAL**

The purpose of this professional development activity is to introduce participants to enrichment clusters and establish the difference between clusters and mini-courses. Review the fundamental differences between enrichment clusters and mini-courses (see Comparison Sheet). Using the large chart on display, talk the assembled group through a sample simulation (see Sample Enrichment Cluster Sheet). Ask the group to call out an interest area that adults may be drawn to. (Remind them to "keep it clean!") As each person offers an interest area (e.g., wine tasting, cooking, travel, fitness, etc.), record it on chart paper and give it to the person who becomes the "holder" of the interest area. Ask that person to stand somewhere in the room and continue until there are enough interest area selections to break the larger group into smaller groups. Ask the participants to choose an interest area that they wish to develop into a cluster and to stand with the "holder" of the interest area. (For this simulation, participants need not be truly intrigued by the interest area.) Provide each group with a Cluster Simulation Worksheet, a colored marker, and a pencil and encourage them to relocate to a comfortable area to work. Give them 20-30 minutes to respond to the seven items on the worksheet and record their answers on chart paper. Ask each group to select a spokesperson that will display the completed chart and share it with the larger group. Leave approximately five minutes for each spokesperson to share. End the session by encouraging participants to think about their experience. The next activity requires them to share what worked in the simulation and what challenges need to be addressed to ensure success.

Note: Between professional development sessions, provide articles about enrichment clusters to interested parties.

Sample Enrichment Cluster Sheet

Topic: Wine Tasting

Title: The Grapes of Wrath Society

Product: Guide to Local Wineries

Authentic Audience: Local Tourist Bureau

Roles: cartographer, graphic designer, artist, researcher, writer, editor, project manager

Resources and methodologies:
                                an interview with a sommelier, books about wine tasting, maps of the region, Internet access, etc.

Skills: an array of geography, technology, layout design, research, writing, organizational, artistic, etc.

Possible Funding Sources:
                                wineries, wine shops, Chamber of Commerce

Note: This simulated enrichment cluster was developed by a group of teachers in a workshop I conducted several years ago.

Comparison Sheet

Some Basic Differences Between Enrichment Clusters and Mini-Courses

ENRICHMENT CLUSTERS	MINI-COURSES
facilitated	taught
crosses grade levels	typically same age peers
action oriented	students learn "stuff"
content emerges through inquiry and action	predetermined content
activity directed toward the production of a product or service	"learning for learning sake"
division of labor	participants usually do the same thing in the same way at the same time
mimics authentic methods of professional investigations	use more generalized teacher-directed research methodologies
product/service geared to an authentic audience	if there is a final project, it may be a basic display, often not seen beyond course participants
transfer of knowledge emphasized	participants acquire knowledge to fulfill course requirements

Cluster Simulation Worksheet

As a group, record the following information:

- Title of Cluster (Team, Company, Ensemble, etc.)

- Resources and Methodologies

- Product or Service

- Roles (Division of Labor)

- Skills (Alignment with Standards, etc.)

- Possible Funding Sources

- Authentic Audience

Choose a spokesperson who will share your cluster with the larger group.

Activity G: Comfort and Concerns with Enrichment Clusters

PURPOSE:	**To share thoughts about enrichment clusters**
TIME:	**Approximately 45 minutes**
SETTING:	**General discussion area**
MATERIALS:	**Chart paper, marker**
DESIGNATION:	**Essential**

After engaging participants in the Enrichment Cluster Simulation, set a date to come together to discuss participants' experiences in the simulation. Begin by asking the assembled group to think about how enrichment clusters align with their beliefs and with what they value for their students. You can begin the process by listing some of your own "comfort starters" (e.g., working with colleagues, interest-based learning, exposing students to real-world work ethics, etc.) Break into smaller groups, making sure that each group includes some "positive" teachers Ask them to continue to list comforts and then shift to concerns. Ask participants to share their top concerns with the whole group, instructing them to listen carefully and avoid repeating any concern that has already been raised. Record all comforts and concerns on chart paper. As the workshop ends tell them that you will provide them with their own list and, at a future meeting, all concerns will be addressed. I recommend following the same post activity procedure described after Activity E (Facing Challenges).

Note: This activity can be modified to address any SEM component.

Activity H: Developing a Checklist for High-end Learning

PURPOSE:	**To enhance professional reflection and the examination of actual samples of student work**
TIME:	**Ongoing**
SETTING:	**Any location where teachers can comfortably meet**
MATERIALS:	**Sample(s) of student work**
DESIGNATION:	**Optional**

Ask teachers to get together with other teachers on their grade level to examine samples of student work that they believe exemplifies high-end learning. Each teacher should bring three samples. Encourage them to discuss criteria for high-end learning. Some questions you can pose to spark their conversation may be: Does the sample represent a superior response to the task? How do you judge what a superior response would be? Is the response representative of the standards or curriculum objectives expected in your state?

Have teachers sort the samples into three piles: Good, Better, and Best. Teachers should first concentrate on the Best pile and pin down a list of attributes apparent in this group. Write a description of each of the attributes. Then working backwards, have teachers take another look at the Good pile and judge what a good response would be. Finally, follow the same process for the Better pile. This process ensures that the Best pile truly stands above the rest. Teachers should design a checklist with no more than ten items to help them assess the presence or absence of the attributes in the Best pile. The more checks a sample has, the closer it is to being a high-end learning sample of student work.

Activity I: Celebrating Student Work That Exemplifies High-end Learning

PURPOSE:	To celebrate high-end learning
TIME:	45-60 minutes
SETTING:	Any space conducive for sharing examples of student work.
MATERIALS:	Sample(s) of student work
DESIGNATION:	Essential

This is a two-session activity. During the first meeting encourage participants to think about how they incorporate high-end learning into their instructional programs. Participants then brainstorm a list of examples and think about student work that reflects high-end learning.

The second session is a celebration of the wonderful high-end learning taking place in your school. Organize participants into small groups that include representatives from each grade level plus special area teachers. Encourage, but do not require, teachers to bring a sample of student work that exemplifies high-end learning to share. After the celebration, you can collect the samples of student work to place in a binder for reference or proudly display on a bulletin board in the school

Activity J: Point/Counterpoint

PURPOSE:	**To prepare for potential reactions from stakeholders when introducing SEM**
TIME:	**Approximately 15 minutes**
SETTING:	**General discussion area**
MATERIALS:	**Paper, markers, overhead projector or flip chart, clipboard for participants (one per group)**
DESIGNATION:	**Optional**

You can use this activity as a self-reflection tool for yourself alone or with other administrators, the SEM Team, or any group charged with the responsibility of successfully implementing SEM. The purpose is to help those responsible for introducing and fostering implementation gauge potential reactions to SEM.

Divide the group in half and ask them to move to opposite ends of the room. Assign one group the role of agreeing with a statement, and the other group will argue against the statement. Explain to them that for the purposes of the activity, they need not personally agree with the argument they will be asked to make. On an overhead projector or flip chart, write the phrase that they will react to: "Providing services for gifted children only is elitist." Allow each group 15 minutes to list their arguments, then record them on the chart. Mix up the group by pairing members of each group together to discuss how to use the arguments to foster implementation.

Use the following list as a reference.

Agree : Providing services for gifted children only *is elitist* because . . .

- they reduce resources for others; funds are disproportionately allocated.
- they lower regular classroom expectations.
- teachers/parents/identified students look down on "regular" students.
- they lower self-esteem of students who are not identified.
- they widen gap between "haves" and "have-nots."
- average students miss out.
- they are divisive.
- they become a special privilege.
- they drain the talent pool.
- they foster negative socialization issues.

Disagree: Providing services for gifted children only *is not elitist* because . . .

- they promote excellence in education.
- they match students' specific learning needs.
- they respond to parent/community concerns (keep parents happy).
- they focus resources on gifted children's needs.
- other students become classroom leaders/rise to the top (because gifted children are

out of the classroom).

- they challenge students ready to be challenged.
- our society needs to develop the potentials of gifted students.
- they provide comfort for students already perceived as different in some way.
- they can reduce underachievement.

Activity K: Developing Artifacts

PURPOSE:	**To find and display evidence of SEM in your school**
TIME:	**Approximately 30-45 minutes**
SETTING:	**Participants at tables**
MATERIALS:	**81/2" X 11" writing paper, 18" x 24" construction paper, pencils, markers, thumb tacks or masking tape, Artifact Siting Form (optional)**
DESIGNATION:	**Essential**

If you are just starting implementation, ask participants to think about examples that would show that SEM is working in their school (press releases, letters to parents, bulletin board display, etc.). Provide some time for them to share their perceptions and then explain that for the next 20 minutes, they will work with their partner to develop at least one artifact that could be used to promote SEM.

If implementation is already underway, ask participants to work with a partner to discuss whether or not they feel that there are examples in your building that the enrichment learning and teaching practices associated with SEM are taking place. They should then locate evidence that SEM is at work in their school.

Ask participants to affix the artifacts (either created or genuine) to the wall around the perimeter of the room. Reorganize participants into small groups, with one group in front of each artifact. After several minutes, allow groups to rotate and view the next artifact. (Arranging the viewing time in this way will allow each individual to see each artifact in a timely manner.) Bring participants back together to discuss the artifacts. What makes some artifacts better examples and good promoters of SEM?

In closing, encourage participants to examine their workspace to determine if SEM products and learning experiences are evident. Remind them that visible proof that the school promotes high-end learning can affect public perceptions. An Artifact Siting Form can help you keep track of the artifacts in your building.

Sample Artifact Siting Form

Artifact: Bulletin Board Photo

Display Site: Second Grade Wing

Date: November 26th

Name or description of artifact: Journey Into American Indian Culture enrichment cluster photographs

Event or contact, if any, with which the artifact is associated: Curriculum-based study of American Indian Culture

Brief summary of artifact's purpose: Students in grade two participated in a curriculum based enrichment cluster program to learn about American Indian culture.

Significance or importance of the artifact: After participating in some introductory mini-lessons, students self-selected areas of study in which they prepared to become "the experts." Students selected from The American Indian Games and Chants Society, The American Indian Culinary Group, The American Indian Arts Guild, and The American Indian Stories and Legends Association. After participating in a five-session grade level cluster experience, students were reorganized into small groups to share their new knowledge with the "other experts." The Journey into American Indian Cultural Fair culminated the experience.

Artifact Siting Form

Artifact: _____

_____

Display Site: _____

_____

Date: _____

Name or description of artifact: _____

_____

_____

Event or contact, if any, with which the artifact is associated: _____

_____

_____

Brief summary of artifact's purpose: _____

_____

_____

_____

Significance or importance of the artifact: _____

_____

_____

_____

_____

Activity L: Public Relations Simulation

PURPOSE:	**To prepare for interview situations**
TIME:	**Approximately 45 minutes**
SETTING:	**Large room**
MATERIALS:	**Interview Simulation Sheets, recording equipment (optional)**
DESIGNATION:	**Optional**

This simulation is designed to help educators learn how to be cautious when dealing with the press. Introduce this activity by explaining to participants that they will role-play an interview situation. Participants will either be an administrator responsible for SEM implementation (Program Director) or an education reporter from the local newspaper. Separate participants into two groups and make sure that each group is out of earshot of other group. Distribute the interview simulation sheet applicable to each group.

Visit the reporter group and explain that their mission in this simulation is to remain friendly and pleasant throughout the interview, but to put a negative spin in the headline for the article they would write. In other words, the administrator should leave the interview feeling great about the interview and confident that a positive headline will result when in fact a negative headline is the outcome. The reporter, while listening to the Program Director's responses, should think of a headline. For example, when hearing that the enrichment program is funded under the umbrella of special education, the resulting headline might be "Gifted Program Takes Funds From Special Education!"

Next visit with the Program Directors to make sure they understand it is their responsibility to tout how great their programs are.

Once participants understand their roles, they should separate into pairs (1 Program Director and 1 Reporter) and spend 15 minutes on the interview. If equipment is available, have each pair record the interview to review at a later time. After the interviews, everyone should comes back together for discussion. Ask for a pair to volunteer to be the first to share what occurred during the interview. First the Program Director should explain what he or she said to the Education Reporter. Then the Education Reporter should read the headline he or she has developed out loud. This process should continue until all of the pairs have presented.

Finally, participants should brainstorm strategies to minimize negative spin (build a relationship with the reporter, encourage students to take part in the interview, be prepared, know the reporter's bias, etc.).

Note: This activity can also be broken down into a two- or three-session activity:

Two-Session	Session One:	Simulation
	Session Two:	Discussion
Three-Session	Session One:	Simulation preparation: provide time for participants to think of possible questions and responses
	Session Two:	Simulation
	Session Three:	Discussion

Directions for the Education Reporter

Your role in this simulation is to create a sensationalized headline that makes the enrichment program the administrator is promoting look bad or the administrator look somewhat less than competent or knowledgeable. In your article, you may choose to harp on a particular theme such as elitism or call attention to a particular activity that you think is of questionable value.

The administrator should have no idea that you intend to sensationalize the news by making generous use of a favorite tactic, quoting people out of context! Your last article appeared under the headline, "Principal Says Gifted Kids Steal Funding From Special Education Students." What the principal actually said was, "Special Education funds in our district now include funds for gifted and talented programming."

Remember that the person playing the administrator's role in this simulation does not know about your intent and has not read this set of instructions. If you are too aggressive in your interview you may cause the administrator to sense your underlying motives and thus become defensive or clam up. A part of your role is to disguise your agenda. Keep in mind that you are an experienced reporter (and former teacher) and therefore know a great deal about the ins and outs of school programs, the jargon of education, and problems that might occur in programs for the gifted and talented.

The administrator can make three off-the-record (OTR) statements. You cannot use these statements in the article, but you can use these statements to guide subsequent questions.

Directions for the Program Director

Pretend you are the administrator of a newly adopted SEM program in a large suburban community. The program has been designed around a pull-out approach, with some general enrichment opportunities at some grade levels.

The gifted program has always been a hot topic in your community. Newspaper articles have been highly influential in generating both support for the program and "fuel for the fire" for critics of (1) gifted education in general, (2) identification practices, and (3) specific curricular approaches and program activities. Your program is coming up for budgetary review and approval at the board of education meeting, and you are scheduled for an interview with a newspaper reporter prior to the meeting. Your statements to the press will carry a great deal of weight in swaying public opinion and board action. Unfortunately, the reporter conducting the interview is the new education editor for the local paper, and you have no idea how this person views gifted programs.

Under these circumstances you will want to be cautious in the interview, and answer all questions as accurately and honestly as possible. Feel free to fabricate anything you would like about your program, including "the enthusiastic support of classroom teachers" and "the outstanding enthusiasm from parents" or anything else that characterizes your idealized program. If you feel particularly threatened or uncertain about some of the questions or issues raised in the interview, you may make a maximum of three "off-the-record" (OTR) statements. The reporter cannot include any of your OTR statements in the article. Be careful, however, because your OTR statements may influence subsequent questions or the general tone of the article. If the reporter makes some particularly outrageous or erroneous statements about your program, you certainly have the right to challenge his/her information or sources.

APPENDIX D: THE SEM ADMINISTRATOR'S LIBRARY

A Rising Tide Lifts All Ships: Developing the Gifts and Talents of All Students by Joseph S. Renzulli. (October 1998). *Phi Delta Kappan*, pp 105-111.

Total School Improvement by Joseph S. Renzulli and Jeanne H. Purcell. (September/October, 1995). *Our Children*, pp. 30-31.

Getting the Word Out: Working with Your Local School Reporter by A. Hennessey. (1992, September). *Phi Delta Kappan*, pp. 82-84.

Interface Between Gifted Education and General Education: Toward Communication, Cooperation and Collaboration by C. A. Tomlinson, M. R. Coleman, S. Allan. (1996). *Gifted Child Quarterly 40*(3), pp. 165-171.

For additional articles, visit the web site for The Neag Center for Gifted Education and Talent Development (www.gifted.uconn.edu).

Books

Curriculum Compacting: The Complete Guide to Modifying the Regular Curriculum for High-Ability Students by Sally M. Reis, Deborah E. Burns, and Joseph S. Renzulli
Curriculum compacting helps teachers streamline the regular curriculum, ensure students' mastery of basic skills, and provide time for challenging enrichment and/or acceleration activities. This book covers everything teachers need to understand, justify, and implement curriculum compacting for advanced learners. *Published by Creative Learning Press, Inc. 888-518-8004; www.creative-learningpress.com*

Developing the Gifts and Talents of All Students in the Regular Classroom: An Innovative Curricular Design Based on the Enrichment Triad Model by Margaret Beecher
Based on the Enrichment Triad Model and principles of differentiation, this curriculum model addresses interest-based teaching, interdisciplinary curriculum, self-directed learning, and more. Specific planning and management techniques show educators how to implement this model effectively and efficiently. *Published by Creative Learning Press, Inc. 888-518-8004; www.creativelearningpress.com*

Enrichment Clusters: A Practical Plan for Real-World, Student-Driven Learning by Joseph S. Renzulli, Marcia Gentry, and Sally M. Reis
Step-by-step guidelines show schools how to set up an enrichment cluster program within the regular school week, train staff and community volunteers, create successful clusters, assess student products, evaluate the program, and more. Easy-to-use staff development activities and dozens of

THE SEM ADMINISTRATOR'S LIBRARY

reproducibles help schools get the program up and running with minimal time and funding. (Includes a reproducible copy of the Inspiration teacher survey.) *Published by Creative Learning Press, Inc. 888-518-8004; www.creativelearningpress.com*

The Fifth Discipline: The Art and Practice of the Learning Organization by P. M. Senge
A must read for every administrator who is interested in building a learning organization, this resource clearly details how to overcome threats to an organization and build upon new opportunities. Senge offers an empowering approach to work and, even though the book was not written specifically for schools, *The Fifth Discipline* will inspire a dramatic shift of mind for any educator in a leadership position. *Published by Doubleday; www.randomhouse.com/doubleday*

The First-Time Grantwriter's Guide to Success by Cynthia Knowles
This clear, concise guide walks readers through each step of the grantwriting process, from finding sources to final submissions. Also included are checklists, sample forms, lists of resources, and a glossary of terms. *Published by Corwin Press. 800-818-7243; www.corwinpress.com*

Getting Results with Curriculum Mapping by Heidi Hayes Jacobs
This book offers a wide range of perspectives on how best to approach the curriculum mapping process. Chapters present great advice on preparing to implement mapping procedures, how to use software to create mapping databases, integrating staff development initiatives through mapping, and much more. *Published by Association for Supervision and Curriculum Development. 800-933-ASCD; www.ascd.org*

How to Get Grants and Gifts for the Public Schools by Stanley Levenson
Author Stanley Levenson presents an overview of different types of grants currently available as well as information on major government funding agencies. Sample grants illustrate successful techniques, and blank application forms for the U. S. Department of Education help schools get started. Readers also learn how to set up a Local Education Foundation and strategies for successfully soliciting from individuals in the community. *Published by Allyn & Bacon. 866-346-7314; www.ablongman.com*

Inspiration (included in *Enrichment Clusters*)
This survey helps teachers identify interests and activities that may be the basis for an enrichment clusters.

Interest-A-Lyzer Family of Instruments by Joseph S. Renzulli
This manual describes the six interest assessment tools that comprise the Interest-A-Lyzer "Family of Instruments." Dr. Renzulli discusses the importance of assessing student interests and provides suggestions for administering and interpreting these instruments in the school setting. Sample pages from each interest assessment tool are included in the appendix. Class sets (30 copies) of the

Interest-A-Lyzer instruments are sold separately. *Published by Creative Learning Press, Inc. 888-518-8004; www.creativelearningpress.com*

It's About Time: Inservice Strategies for Curriculum Compacting by Alane J. Starko
This practical guide describes curriculum compacting procedures and provides step-by-step guidelines for conducting inservice presentations on curriculum compacting. The book includes information about methods for compacting the regular curriculum, techniques for assessing mastery, simulation activities, blackline masters for inservice training, and more. *Published by Creative Learning Press, Inc. 888-518-8004; www.creativelearningpress.com*

Mapping the Big Picture: Integrating Curriculum and Assessment K-12 by Heidi Hayes Jacobs.
To help curriculum committees get a clear picture of what is happening in classrooms, Jacobs presents a seven-step process for mapping the curriculum. The maps help educators examine curricula in specific classrooms, a school, or even a district at specific points during the school year. Hayes Jacobs offers more than 20 sample maps that illustrate how to streamline the curriculum by closing gaps and removing redundancies. *Published by the Association for Supervision and Curriculum Development. 800-933-ASCD; www.ascd.org*

The Multiple Menu Model: A Practical Guide for Developing Differentiated Curriculum by Joseph S. Renzulli, Jann H. Leppien, and Thomas S. Hays
The Multiple Menu Model helps curriculum developers and teachers challenge learners on all levels and make learning more meaningful, relevant, and engaging. Teachers learn how to locate a topic in the realm of knowledge and uncover basic principles, concepts, and methodologies; address issues of balance between content and process objectives; apply teaching strategies; organize and sequence a unit or lesson; determine a range of outcomes; and inject personal creative contributions into the lesson. *Published by Creative Learning Press, Inc. 888-518-8004; www.creativelearningpress.com*

The Parallel Curriculum: A Design to Develop High Potential and Challenge High-Ability Learners by Carol Ann Tomlinson, Sandy N. Kaplan, Joseph S. Renzulli, Deborah E. Burns, Jann H. Leppien, and Jeanne H. Purcell
Four parallel approaches to curriculum development illustrate ascending intellectual demand as a means of extending the intensity of challenge for students as they work toward expertise in learning. This guide provides practical guidelines for developing curricula in all classrooms that ensure rich learning options for all students. *Published by Corwin Press. 800-818-7243; www.corwinpress.com*

Reframing Organizations: Artistry, Choice and Leadership (2nd edition) by Lee G. Bolman and Terrence E. Deal.
By examining real-life situations through multiple lenses, Bolman and Deal show how the same situation can be viewed in at least four different ways. Administrators will surely gain insights into how to create effective relationships and instill greater motivation among staff. *Published by Jossey-*

Schools for Talent Development: A Practical Plan for Total School Improvement by Joseph S. Renzulli.

Dr. Renzulli discusses the rationale underlying schoolwide enrichment and the Schoolwide Enrichment Model and the organizational and service delivery components of SEM. Also included are in-depth discussions about enrichment clusters, grouping, talent portfolios, curriculum modifications, and enrichment learning and teaching. *Published by Creative Learning Press, Inc. 888-518-8004; www.creativelearningpress.com*

The Schoolwide Enrichment Model: A How-to Guide for Educational Excellence (2nd Ed.) by Joseph S. Renzulli and Sally M. Reis

In its second edition, *The Schoolwide Enrichment Model* contains updated information about how to achieve educational excellence in today's schools. The guide offers practical, step-by-step advice for implementing successful SEM programs in the K-12 school setting, discusses schoolwide enrichment, and provides information about the model's school structures, organizational components, and service delivery. It includes a collection of useful instruments, checklists, charts, taxonomies, assessment tools, forms, and planning guides that are designed to help educators find effective ways to organize, administer, maintain, and evaluate different aspects of the Schoolwide Enrichment Model. *Published by Creative Learning Press, Inc. 888-518-8004; www.creativelearningpress.com*

Thinking Smart: A Primer for the Talents Unlimited Model edited by Carol Schlichter and W. Ross Palmer

Based on Calvin Taylor's multiple talent theory, the Talents Unlimited Model is designed to develop creative and critical thinking skills. The book addresses theory, research, classroom and school application, and evaluations. *Published by Creative Learning Press, Inc. 888-518-8004; www.creativelearningpress.com*

Total Talent Portfolio: A Systematic Plan to Identify and Nurture Gifts and Talents by Jeanne H. Purcell and Joseph S. Renzulli

A component of the Schoolwide Enrichment Model, this book presents a systematic vehicle for gathering and recording information on students to develop a total picture of a student's talents, interests, and abilities. Portfolios help teachers analyze each student's unique talent profile and decide which types of enrichment and acceleration options will be most likely to develop each young person's talents and abilities. Sample portfolios are included as well as suggestions for developing your own. *Published by Creative Learning Press, Inc. 888-518-8004; www.creativelearningpress.com*

Videos

A Rising Tide Lifts All Ships

This twelve-minute videotape introduces educators, administrators, and parents to the Schoolwide Enrichment Model and offers basic information on how they can help develop the gifts and talents of all students. *Distributed by Creative Learning Press, Inc. 888-518-8004; www.creativelearningpress.com*

Fish! Sticks

Fish! Catch the Energy, Release the Potential

These short videos describe how a sleepy little fish market in Seattle becomes world famous when employees develop a vision. Both videos are approximately 17 minutes long. *Produced and distributed by Charthouse International Learning Corporation. 800-328-3789; www.fishphilosophy.com / www.charthouse.com*

Web Sites

The Neag Center for Gifted Education and Talent Development: www.gifted.uconn.edu

The National Association for Gifted Children: www.nagc.org

The National Research Center on the Gifted and Talented: www.gifted.uconn.edu/nrcgt.html

APPENDIX E: SUMMARY OF RESEARCH ON SEM AND RELATED MODELS

Summary of Research on SEM and Related Models[*]

STUDY	SAMPLES	MAJOR FINDING
Curriculum Compacting		
Imbeau, M. (1991). *Teachers' attitudes toward curriculum compacting: A comparison of different inservice strategies.* Unpublished doctoral dissertation. University of Connecticut, Storrs, CT.	Primary (K-2) Elementary (3-5) Middle (6-8) Secondary (9-12)	Group membership (peer coaching) was a significant predictor of post-test teachers' attitudes.
Reis, S. M., Westberg, K. L., Kulikowich, J. M., and Purcell, J. H. (1998). Curriculum compacting and achievement test scores: What does the research say? *Gifted Child Quarterly, 42*(2), 123-129.	Elementary (3-5) Middle (6-8)	Using curriculum compacting to eliminate 40%–50% of curricula for students with demonstrated advanced content knowledge and superior ability resulted in no decline in achievement test scores.
Effectiveness of SEM as Perceived by Teachers, Administrators, and Parents		
Reis, S. M. (1981). *An analysis of the productivity of gifted students participating in programs using the Revolving Door Identification Model.* Unpublished doctoral dissertation. University of Connecticut, Storrs, CT.	Primary (K-2) Elementary (3-5)	Teachers preferred the Revolving Door identification procedures over more traditional methods of identification; teachers reported that a high level of involvement with the program influenced their teaching practices.
Olenchak, F. R. (1988). The schoolwide enrichment model in the elementary schools: A study of implementation stages and effects on educational excellence. In J. S. Renzulli (Ed.), *Technical report on research studies relating to the Revolving Door Identification Model* (2nd ed.). Storrs, CT: Bureau of Educational Research, The University of Connecticut.	Elementary (3-5)	SEM contributed to improved teachers', parents', and administrators' attitudes toward education for high-ability students.
Cooper, C. (1983). *Administrators' attitudes toward gifted programs based on the enrichment triad/revolving door identification model: Case studies in decision-making.* Unpublished doctoral dissertation, The University of Connecticut, Storrs, CT.	8 districts	Administrator perceptions regarding the model included greater staff participation in education of high ability students, more positive staff attitudes toward the program, fewer concerns about identification, positive changes in how the guidance department worked with students, more incentives for students to work toward higher goals.

[*] Adapted from Renzulli, J. S. (1994). *Schools for talent development: A practical plan for total school improvement.* Mansfield Center, CT: Creative Learning Press and *Research related to the Schoolwide Enrichment Model* (n.d.). Retrieved August 17, 2004 from University of Connecticut, Neag Center for Gifted Education and Talent Development Web Site: http://www.gifted. uconn.edu/sem/rrsem.html

STUDY	SAMPLES	MAJOR FINDING
Friedman, N. (2001). *Policy implications for the implementation of the Schoolwide Enrichment Model.* Unpublished doctoral dissertation. Hofstra University, Hempstead, NY.	Administrators	Administrators tend to implement SEM in one of three patterns: Mandated, Collaborative, and Blended. The qualities inherent in each of these patterns might have exacerbated or minimized the volatility of issues relative to SEM and led to policy implications for implementation.
Creativity and SEM–Quality of Products		
Reis, S. M. (1981). *An analysis of the productivity of gifted students participating in programs using the Revolving Door Identification Model.* Unpublished doctoral dissertation. University of Connecticut, Storrs, CT.	Primary (K-2) Elementary (3-5)	Products of above average students were equally as good as products completed by students who were identified for the program using traditional methods.
Gubbins, E. J. (1982). *Revolving door identification model: Characteristics of talent pool students.* Unpublished doctoral dissertation, The University of Connecticut, Storrs, CT.	Elementary (3-5)	Students who did not generate self-selected projects (Type IIIs) attributed the lack of product development to time management difficulties and difficulty in generating product ideas.
Creativity and SEM–Effects of Training		
Burns, D. E. (1987). *The effects of group training activities on students' creative productivity.* Unpublished doctoral dissertation, The University of Connecticut, Storrs, CT.	Elementary (3-5)	Students receiving process skill training were 64% more likely to initiate self-selected projects (Type IIIs) than the students who did not receive the training.
Newman, J. L. (1991). *The effects of the talents unlimited model on students' creative productivity.* Unpublished doctoral dissertation, The University of Alabama, Tuscaloosa, AL.	Elementary (3-5)	Students with training in the Talents Unlimited Model were more likely to complete independent investigations (Type IIIs) than students who did not receive the training.
SEM and Creativity–Investigations of Student Creative and Productive Behaviors		
Delcourt, M. A. B. (1988). *Characteristics related to high levels of creative/productive behavior in secondary school students: A multi-case study.* Unpublished doctoral dissertation, The University of Connecticut, Storrs, CT.	Secondary (9-12)	Students completing self-selected investigations (Type IIIs) displayed positive changes in the following: personal skills required for project completion (e.g., writing), personal characteristics (e.g., increased patience), and decisions related to career choices.

STUDY	SAMPLES	MAJOR FINDING
Starko, A. J. (1986). *The effects of the revolving door identification model on creative productivity and self-efficacy.* Unpublished doctoral dissertation, The University of Connecticut, Storrs, CT.	Elementary (3-5)	Students who became involved with self-selected independent studies in SEM programs initiated their own creative products both inside and outside school more often than students who qualified for the program but did not receive services. Students in the enrichment group completed over twice as many creative projects per student (3.37) as the comparison group (.50) and showed greater diversity and sophistication in projects. The number of creative products completed in school (Type IIIs) was a highly significant predictor of self-efficacy.
SEM and Personal and Social Development		
Olenchak, F. R. (1991). Assessing program effects for gifted/learning disabled students. In R. Swassing & A. Robinson (Eds.), *NAGC 1991 research briefs.* Washington, DC: National Association for Gifted Students.	Elementary (3-5)	Supported use of SEM as a means of meeting educational needs of a wide variety of high ability students. SEM, when used as an intervention, was associated with improved attitudes toward learning among elementary, high ability students with learning disabilities. Furthermore, the same students, who completed a high percentage of Type III projects, made positive gains with respect to self-concept.
SEM and Social Acceptability		
Skaught, B. J. (1987). *The social acceptability of talent pool students in an elementary school using the schoolwide enrichment model.* Unpublished doctoral dissertation, The University of Connecticut, Storrs, CT.	Elementary (3-5)	Students identified as above average for a SEM program were positively accepted by their peers. In schools where SEM had been implemented, a "condition of separateness" did not exist for students in the program.

STUDY	SAMPLES	MAJOR FINDING
Heal, M. M. (1989). *Student perceptions of labeling the gifted: A comparative case study analysis.* Unpublished doctoral dissertation, The University of Connecticut, Storrs, CT.	Elementary (3-5)	SEM was associated with a reduction in the negative effects of labeling.
SEM and Underachievement		
Emerick, L. J. (1988). *Academic underachievement among the gifted: Students' perceptions of factors relating to the reversal of academic underachievement patterns.* Unpublished doctoral dissertation, The University of Connecticut, Storrs, CT.	Secondary (9-12)	Reasons for reversal of academic underachievement attributed to various components of SEM, including curriculum compacting, exposure to Type I experiences, opportunities to be involved in Type III studies, and an appropriate assessment of learning styles to provide a match between students and teacher.
Baum, S., Renzulli, J. S., & Hébert, T. P. (1995). *The prism metaphor: A new paradigm for reversing underachievement* (Research Monograph No. CRS95310). Storrs, CT: The National Research Center on the Gifted and Talented, University of Connecticut.	Elementary (3-5) Middle (6-8)	A positive gain in classroom performance was made by underachieving students who undertook a self-selected independent investigation (Type III).
Taylor, L. A. (1992). *The effects of the secondary enrichment triad model on the career development of vocational-technical school students.* Unpublished doctoral dissertation, The University of Connecticut, Storrs, CT.	Secondary (9-12)	Involvement in Type III studies substantially increased post-secondary education plans of students (from attending 2.6 years to attending 4.0 years).
SEM and High Ability/Learning Disabled Students		
Baum, S. (1988). An enrichment program for gifted learning disabled students. *Gifted Child Quarterly, 32*(1), 226-230.	Elementary (3-5)	The Type III independent study, when used as an intervention with high ability, learning disabled students, was associated with improvement in the students' behavior, specifically the ability to self-regulate time on task, improvement in self-esteem, and the development of specific instructional strategies to enhance the potential of high potential, learning disabled students.

STUDY	SAMPLES	MAJOR FINDING
SEM and Self-Efficacy		
Schack, G. D. (1986). *Creative productivity and self-efficacy in children.* Unpublished doctoral dissertation, The University of Connecticut, Storrs, CT.	Elementary (3-5) Middle (6-8)	Self-efficacy was a significant predictor of initiation of an independent investigation, and self-efficacy at the end of treatment was higher in students who participated in Type III projects.
Starko, A. (1986). *The effects of the revolving door identification model on creative productivity and self-efficacy.* Unpublished doctoral dissertation, The University of Connecticut, Storrs, CT.	Elementary (3-5)	Students who became involved with self-selected independent studies in SEM programs initiated their own creative products both inside and outside school more often than students who qualified for the program but did not receive services. Students in the enrichment group reported over twice as many creative projects per student (3.37) as the comparison group (.50) and showed greater diversity and sophistication in projects. The number of creative products completed in school (Type IIIs) was a highly significant predictor of self-efficacy.
SEM and Longitudinal Research		
Delcourt, M. A. B. (1993). Creative productivity among secondary school students: Combining energy, interest, and imagination. *Gifted Child Quarterly, 37*(1), 23-31.	Longitudinal	Students who participated in Type III projects, both in and out of school, maintained interests in college and career aspirations that were similar to those manifested during their public school years as opposed to previous reports of little or no relation between personally initiated and assigned school projects.
Hébert, T. P. (1993). Reflections at graduation: The long-term impact of elementary school experiences in creative productivity. *Roeper Review, 16*(1), 22-28.	Longitudinal	Type III interests of students affect post-secondary plans. A decrease in creative Type III productivity occurs during junior high. Creative outlets are needed in high school. The Type III process serves as important training for later productivity.

APPENDIX F: COMMONLY USED TERMS

Commonly Used Terms

Students with **above average ability** refers to students who have tested in the superior range on achievement and or intelligence measures (Renzulli, 1978).

Academies of Inquiry are enrichment clusters at the middle school level.

At-risk students are those who may underachieve or who may drop out of school. Unmet economic, physical, emotional, linguistic, and/or academic needs may inhibit a student's ability to learn or attend school (Ward, 1998).

Creativity is the process of combining what exists into something new. The something new could be a procedure, idea, or product relative to the individual, or it can mean the human attribute of constructive originality (Ward, 1998).

Elitism (Elitist) advocates the selection and treatment of people as superior in some way who are therefore favored (Ward, 1998).

Enrichment experiences or activities are those that are above and beyond what are usually included within the grade level curriculum. Falling under the general term enrichment are such practices and offerings as special assignments, independent study, mini-courses, etc. (Renzulli & Reis, 1997).

Enrichment Learning and Teaching is a systematic set of strategies designed to promote active engagement in learning on the parts of both teachers and students (Renzulli & Reis, 1997).

Equity provides fair and impartial learning opportunities and access to good teaching for all students. In order to meet educational needs at all levels of development, these opportunities should encourage and enable all students to develop to their fullest potential (Ward, 1998).

Giftedness is viewed as an interaction among three basic clusters of human traits (above average general abilities, high levels of task commitment, and high levels of creativity) (Renzulli, 1978).

Gifted behaviors are behaviors that emerge when above average ability, task commitment, and creativity interact with one another in relation to a particular topic, area of interest, or specific talent. A person may be described as displaying a specific talent when she or he is intensely involved in a task-specific activity and is able to produce a new piece of knowledge, insight, or product within her or his chosen area of interest (Renzulli, 1978).

Gifted education is a compilation of instructional models and an array of teaching strategies that are concept driven rather than fact driven, instruct students in the skills of discovery, research, independence, group cooperation, inquiry, and creativity, and then apply these skills to a broad range of disciplines (Tomlinson & Callahan, 1992).

A **gifted and talented student** is a child enrolled in an elementary, middle, or secondary school identified as possessing demonstrated or potential abilities that give evidence of high performance capability as defined by a local definition (California Education Code 52201).

Interest-A-Lyzer is an instrument that assists students in examining their potential interests (Renzulli, 1997).

The **Schoolwide Enrichment Model** is a systematic set of specific strategies for increasing student effort, enjoyment, and performance and for integrating a broad range of advanced level learning experiences and higher order thinking skills into any curricular area, course of study, or pattern of school organization (Renzulli & Reis, 1985, 1997).

Task commitment reflects an individual's energy that is brought to bear on a particular problem or specific performance area (Renzulli, 1978).

Three-Ring Conception of Giftedness is the theoretical framework underlying Renzulli's theory of giftedness (Renzulli, 1978).

Index

T

W

About the Author

Nora G. Friedman, Ed. D., has worked in schools as a classroom teacher, enrichment specialist, and building administrator implementing or considering implementing the Schoolwide Enrichment Model. She is the principal of the South Grove Elementary School in the Syosset School District, New York, and mentor to a team of enrichment specialists across the district. Nora has been a Strand Coordinator at Confratute for fifteen years, working with central office and building level administrators wishing to implement the model. She earned a doctorate in education at Hofstra University, focusing her work on the policy implications for implementing this model. Each year, Nora teaches a graduate course at Hofstra University, Instructional Methods and Materials for Exceptional High Ability Learners. She is a member of the Board of Directors of Talents Unlimited, representing Talents Unlimited Certified Trainers nationwide.